Death Of
A Country

Death Of
A Country

The Civil War in Lebanon

JOHN
BULLOCH

Weidenfeld and Nicolson
London

Contents

AUTHOR'S NOTE

No attempt has been made in this book to give a scholarly transliteration of Arabic names for people or places. The style adopted is the one generally used in British or French newspapers, which it is thought would be most familiar to readers of this work in the English language.

ACKNOWLEDGEMENTS

The author and publisher would like to thank the following agencies for permission to reproduce their copyright photographs:
Camera Press: 1, 3, 5, 6, 8, 10, 13, 17, 18; Keystone Press: 9, 12, 14 (left), 19; Planet News: 11; United Press International: 15 (right); Associated Press: 16.

They would also like to thank Z. K. Karbowski who drew the maps.

Preface

The Lebanese civil war of 1975 and 1976 cost more than 40,000 lives, devastated vast areas of towns and countryside, and destroyed Beirut as the business and financial centre of the Middle East. It ended with the occupation of this traditionally neutral country by a foreign army with the agreement and connivance of the Great Powers and the other Arab states. And when it did finally come to a close, little appeared to have been gained, for the demands for reform put forward by the Left-wing alliance led by Kamal Jumblatt were not guaranteed, the battle by the Christian Phalangist Party to maintain the special status of the Maronite community in the country did not appear to have been successful, and the Palestinians, though they had not been able to stand up to the might of the invading Syrian armies, still existed as a coherent organization with their leaders in place, their command structure undisturbed, and their weapons and armaments still available. The Syrians, for their part, were spending £1 million a day on a war not of their own making, they were deploying troops and armour on the soil of a brother Arab nation rather than against the Israeli enemy which all Arabs professed to want to fight, and were doing all this not on their own behalf but at the behest of the Arab League.

This was the outward picture; the reality was very different. For the Lebanese conflict was much more than a civil war, though this was an important enough factor. It was also a struggle for the leadership of the Arab world, a sorting-out of alliances, and a preparation for the general Middle East settlement which the Arabs were increasingly coming to see as the only hope of getting away from the preoccupation with Israel which was making economic development so difficult.

1

Certainly the war which raged over every inch of Lebanese territory for almost two years was a civil war: it pitted neighbour against neighbour in the classic horror of such affairs, occasionally even divided families, and spared no-one. Its domestic origins lay in the national convention that followed the independence of Lebanon in 1943, an apparently far-sighted agreement between all the communities in Lebanon which apportioned a fair share of power to each. Lebanon had always been an agglomeration of mini-states rather than a country; it was more feudal than its neighbours, despite the sophistication of Beirut; a man was identified by his home village, the name of the clan chief to whom he owed allegiance and, above all, by his religion. Religion in Lebanon had become a badge of politics; to pray in a church or to go to a mosque was as much a political action as voting in an election. The founding fathers, who in their wisdom had sought to devise a scheme by which all could live in harmony, had in fact laid the seeds of the conflict, as each community tried to adapt the system to its own advantage. The Maronites, the largest single group at the time of independence, were given the lion's share; the Shia, a small, poor, primitive group in 1943, were not content with that position in 1976, while the Maronites still wanted to hold on to their advantages. These basic discontents were reinforced by all that had happened over the years: the Maronites in particular and the Christians in general had amassed a disproportionate share of the country's capital, and, though they often used it with paternal benevolence in their feudal homes, when they moved to the cities they refused to do so. Wealth was flaunted in ostentatious consumption, conspicuous luxury was obvious beside appalling poverty, and no heed was paid by the rich and successful to the increasingly strident demands of the poor and dispossessed.

So the scene was set for civil strife: all that was needed was a catalyst or an outside force which would tip the scale. The influx of Palestinian refugees to Lebanon provided both. From 1948 onwards the Palestinians fled from their homeland in the face of Israeli conquest or harassment, or merely through fear. First they stopped on the West Bank; then, as that was overrun, they moved into Jordan proper; and, after King Hussein's bloody re-establishment of his authority in 1970 and 1971,

2

Lebanon was the only haven the Palestinians could find, the only base from which their commandoes could conduct operations against Israel, and the only country in which they could set up their offices, distribute their propaganda and conduct their interminable debates. Some 300,000 Palestinians eventually made Lebanon their home, more than 100,000 of them in the squalid conditions of the fifteen refugee camps dotted around the country, with five of them ringing Beirut and effectively controlling all ways into and out of the capital. Such an influx was bound to cause trouble in a country where the relative numerical strength of the Christian and Moslem communities was a subject of bitter political argument, but the Palestinians refused to pay any heed to the strains and anxieties caused by their presence. Their attitude was officially that they did not interfere in Lebanese affairs, and they could not see that their very presence was an interference. They certainly wanted no part in any internal conflict: their aim was to have a base from which to wage their campaign for the restoration of their homeland. The trouble was that the preservation of such a base meant they had to take action against those they considered likely to harm them. Against their will and inclination, their policies drew them inexorably into conflict with the Lebanese Right, who feared their growing power and saw them as an army of occupation, and into alliance with the Lebanese Left.

This Leftist grouping in Lebanon was largely Moslem, just as the Christians were largely of the Right. There were historical reasons for this, as well as modern pressures: the fertile Mount Lebanon, the Kesrouan with its outlets to the sea, had always been the Maronite heartland, and a thriving community had been built up there of successful farmers, enterprising traders and, above all, middlemen of all kinds willing to act for anyone who visited their shores and anyone from the interior who sought their help. This prosperous region was a contrast to the surrounding areas; the Akkar to the North was still a primitive land of subsistence farmers where blood feuds were carried on from one generation to another; the Bekaa, once the granary of the Roman Empire, was also a district of successful farmers, but it was the Maronite wholesalers who fixed the prices and arranged distribution; Beirut was a city shared by all communities, but one in which the Christians had the largest share of business and commerce, as events were to show; in the South, the Shia peasants were left at the mercy of Israel and the elements.

Into this situation the Palestinians intruded. Already such men as Kamal Jumblatt, the millionaire landowner who espoused the causes of the poor, were drawing the attention of the people to the injustices which existed, the inequalities which were always there. Jumblatt and his allies were making headway against the old conservative feudal Sunni Moslem politicians such as Abdullah Yafi, Saeb Salam or the Solh family, and then another dissident, the powerful Imam Moussa Sad'r, made his appearance to show that the hold of such Shia traditionalists as Kamal Assad could also be broken. The Maronites, in the form of the Phalangist Party, saw the possibilities: if the Palestinians were not subjugated quickly, they would provide the muscle which the growing Leftist movement lacked. So, from 1969 onwards, when the first open clashes between the Palestinians and the Right occurred, the Phalangist aim was clear: the Palestinians had to be stopped; if possible they should be sent out of the country, dispersed through all the Arab states and not concentrated into one. If that was not possible then they had to be 'controlled'. For their part, the Palestinians recognized the dangers and sought an agreement with the Right and with the Lebanese State which would allow them the peaceful haven they sought. For a time it worked: there was an uneasy accommodation which allowed the Palestinians to consolidate their position and build up their strength; and it was this very success which led to their downfall.

For outside forces were in play too. In the years before 1973 the Syrians saw in the Palestinians a useful irregular arm of their own power, and so supported and supplied them, while at the same time trying to exert control through their domination of Saiqa, militarily the most powerful of the commando groups, which was under the direct orders of Syrian Army Intelligence. In 1973 a large section of the Syrian Army command believed they had been let down by the Egyptians and this feeling became widespread after 1975, when President Anwar Sadat formally concluded a deal by which Israel returned to

Egypt a section of Sinai, including the Abu Rudeis oilfield, in return for an Egyptian commitment not to go to war. In the Syrian view, the Egyptians had put economic advantage before the general Arab good, political expediency before the imperative of regaining all Arab lands. There were others besides the Syrians who took the same view, so it was natural for President Hafez Assad, the pragmatic Syrian leader who had brought stability to his country after twenty years of upheavals, to be tempted by the opportunity of seeking the leadership of the whole Arab world. But more important still from the point of view of Damascus was the need to build some credible new bloc which would permit negotiations with Israel to be conducted from a position of reasonable strength. The answer Assad found was the formation of a new northern alliance comprising Jordan, Syria, and the Palestinians with the implicit assumption that at some time in the future Iraq would also join. However, if the Palestinians were to be a part of this alliance, they had to be under Syrian control; so it became necessary for Syria to stop them gaining the outright victory in Lebanon which at one stage seemed possible. If the Palestinians had won, they would have installed a Leftist government in Beirut which they would have controlled, and in such a situation they would have had Syria at their mercy, for they could then have arranged a confrontation with Israel at any time which suited them, rather than at a moment convenient to the Syrians. This was a situation President Assad could not allow to occur; the prospect of a 'wild' government in Lebanon which, at the least, would soon present Israel with an excuse for action (if it did not move itself), could not be tolerated. The old *status quo* had been preferable to this; even a full-scale Right-wing domination by the Phalangist Party would not be so bad, though what Syria would really have liked was a moderate government willing to be 'guided' by Damascus. So Syria switched sides and began supporting the Christian Right, hesitantly at first, then with increasing confidence as it became clear that, despite all their strong words, the only other Arab states which really mattered shared Syria's view of the situation. Encouraged by the implicit support of his peers, President Assad pressed ahead and finally obtained the mandate of the Arab League for the complete occupation of Beirut and the rest of Lebanon which brought the civil war to an end. Only then did it become clear that Syria had, in fact, obtained the best it could have hoped for: under President Elias Sarkis it was obvious that any government installed in Beirut would be completely under Syrian 'tutelage', in the Arab phrase, and subject to the whims of Damascus.

The one factor which allowed Syria to act as it did was American support. From the beginning of 1976 onwards, the Syrians and Americans were as one, were clear about their objectives and had a formal understanding of what each was to do: the Syrian task was to provide the physical force, to move in and to subjugate the warring parties – in particular, the Palestinians. The Americans acted much more discreetly, but in a role no less important. Their part was to see that Israel did not over-react or cause such trouble that other Powers felt able or bound to become involved. The Americans also helped with inter-Arab diplomacy, putting pressure on certain states not to interfere and seeing to it that the feudal Gulf Rulers, who were America's closest allies, did not upset things because of their deep-seated fears of 'radical' Syria. The United States Sixth Fleet in the Mediterranean was also deployed to counter any Russian threat, though none was ever made. The Soviets, on this occasion, were left nearly helpless, as they were in the worst position any Great Power could find itself in: impotent spectators as two of their client states fought it out in an area of vital interest to them. Russia was supplying both Syria and the Palestinians with equipment, and had compelling reasons for continuing its support of both: Syria was its last foothold in the East Mediterranean after the expulsion of the Soviets from Egypt, and the Palestinians were useful as a 'ginger group' and a force which could be unleashed at will to keep the Middle East pot boiling whenever Moscow policy required it. So, making the best of a bad job, the Russians did very little and never became involved on the ground, as they might have done in different circumstances.

The actions of the other Arab states were always in response to what Syria was doing, and none of them was ever able to take any initiative. Egypt had to oppose President Assad because Sadat wanted to hold on to his position as leader of the Arab world, and so he paid lip-service to the commando

6

movement and condemned Syrian interference; at one time, the Egyptians even facilitated the transit of Iraqi troops to Lebanon to fight on the side of the Palestinians, for Iraq, because of its longstanding ideological dispute with Syria, naturally supported the Resistance Movement. But Egypt, in fact, was delighted to see the Palestinians being brought under control; the main objective of Egyptian policy was to secure an overall settlement of the Middle East crisis which would allow President Sadat to devote all his efforts to the development of his own country, beset by huge economic problems. No settlement was possible as long as the Palestinian problem remained unsettled; and one way of resolving it was to turn the Palestinians into vassals of Syria, forced to accept any crumbs the Arab states threw them, rather than being a powerful force in their own right, able to demand things the Arab countries were not at all eager to give.

Inside the Lebanon, all these forces were at work. Iraq and Libya were the main supporters and suppliers of the commandoes, while the unlikely combination of Syria and Israel were their opponents – Israel became the main arms supplier to the Phalangists, a relationship brokered by the C.I.A. In the last weeks of the war Israel was forced to act more openly than at any time in the previous two years, as it realized that time was running out. Israeli tanks and armoured cars were sent to help Phalangists in the South fighting from their bases in the Christian village of Rmeich, and Israeli ships hastily transported reinforcements from Jounieh to Haifa to be sent north to help in the task of clearing the border area of Palestinians. The Israelis were determined not to allow the state of unrest which had existed along the frontier for years past to re-emerge, and Syrian inaction showed that President Assad, too, had no desire to see any wild guerrillas occupying the area, as they might then pose a threat to his carefully planned policies.

When the war ended with complete Syrian domination of the country, it seemed to many inside Lebanon that the 40,000 killed had died in vain. None of the original objectives appeared to have been achieved, the country was devastated, Beirut was in ruins, its position as a financial centre gone, and its people dispersed. Yet a decisive change had been made: the

Palestinians had been cut down to size. The Resistance Movement was still in being, and it still had weapons and leaders, but it could move only by permission of Syria. The Palestinians had become dependents, while the Christian Right, which emerged victorious by Syrian force of arms, was in the most anomalous position. The Phalangists and the N.L.P. had been fighting to maintain their own special position in the Lebanese State and to avoid domination by the Left supported by the Palestinians. They wanted, in effect, to remain 'a special case' in the Arab world. But at the end, they found themselves in a country dominated by Syria, a militantly Arab State, which though it might be willing to accord them a position of privilege would regard them as an interesting minority, not a power in their own right. Lebanon, like it or not, was certainly destined to become part of the Arab world from which it had held aloof for so long.

The people who gained most, though they were slow to realize it, were the Lebanese Left. Kamal Jumblatt himself was not popular with the Syrians, not least because there was a sizeable Druze population in Syria along the border with Lebanon, and Jumblatt might be able to cause trouble there if he wanted to do so. But apart from Jumblatt, the Left seemed bound to get most of what they wanted: an Arab identity for Lebanon, reforms of the system and socialist policies. In a neat twist, the only real trouble for the Left was that they seemed likely to get a system further to the Left than they favoured. Syrian overlordship was certainly not compatible with the rather wishy-washy socialism of Jumblatt and his allies, and it was clear that the Syrians did not intend to give up their control of Lebanon with any great speed.

So, at the end, what did the Lebanese war achieve? Above all, it cleared the way for a general Middle Eastern settlement, and to a degree it put Israel in a worse position than before. The prospects of settlement were improved because the Palestinians would no longer be in a position to torpedo any accord reached, and the public Syrian hanging of those who tried a guerrilla attack in Damascus was an indication of the short shrift the Arabs intended to give to any of the extremist groups who turned to outright terror as a weapon of policy. Israel's position was made worse because it now had the Syrian Army on another front and because it was faced by the prospect of a new alliance on its northern border, while Egypt had been reluctantly forced to back away from its total commitment to peace.

As the Syrians tightened their hold on the country, all the indications were that a general peace was slightly nearer than it had been two years earlier. There were few certainties: the first was that the old Lebanon had gone for good, and nothing remotely similar to that land of strident capitalism was ever likely to appear again. In all probability, a devolved form of government would emerge in which local authorities in a series of cantons would have considerable power, with a weak government at the centre. In this way Syria, which would also exert a strong influence on the policies of the administration in Beirut, would have close control on the ground of the border areas of the Akkar and Bekaa; Israel would retain its domination of the South; the Maronites would be left to their own devices in the Kesrouan, the Druze in the Chouf, and the Palestinians in a coastal enclave between Beirut and Sidon.

The second certainty was that the losers in the civil war were both the Palestinians and the Lebanese, the people who had fought each other so desperately for so long. The Palestinians lost their independence, their power and the prospect of any early establishment of their own state.

The Lebanese lost their country.

1

The battle of Kantari

It had been a bad night and a bad day, and now it was night again. For hours past the mortars had been smashing in at the rate of one every thirty seconds, killing anyone within fifteen yards, gouging holes in roofs, shattering walls and windows. Rockets swished over the roofs from both sides, the explosive B101s that burst as they hit, and the deadly 102s that acted like an armour-piercing shell, cutting a neat hole through a concrete wall, then blowing up inside a building to spread devastation and wreckage. Lazy balls of red tracer arced across the sky, one cartridge in each four, as the gunners pointed out targets to their comrades – and only incidentally killed a few people in the process. And constantly the staccato bark of the AK47s, the basic Russian assault rifle used by the Palestinians and the Left, and the sharper sound of the American M16s with which the Right was armed.

A red glow lit the heart of the city as a building burnt, but most apartments were in darkness as people switched off their lights to avoid attention and sat terror-stricken in whichever rooms they thought safest. No cars moved through the streets, though it was still early evening, and no pedestrians were to be seen. But occasionally light gleamed on a rifle barrel as a watcher shifted his position in a doorway, a man crouched low with his gun at the ready ran across a street, or sidled quietly along a wall to have a word with the next man in the line of defence.

Then, as full darkness fell, suddenly all was action and movement. The men stayed at their places, but from every house came the women and children. Elderly ladies in the traditional sombre black they always wear came out with shovels and dust-pans, trowels used in their roof-top gardens, or anything else of service. Quickly they moved over to the two building sites nearby and began filling the sandbags held by the children. Then the boys took them off in commandeered wheelbarrows to the men on the street corners, and within minutes new barricades were going up. The sandbags were reinforced with building blocks, cement sacks – anything which looked as if it might stop a bullet. And then, as suddenly as they had emerged, the women and children hurried back into their homes, and again the roads were left to the men with the guns.

An hour passed, an hour of watching and waiting, nervous shifting from one foot to another, a clicking on and off of safety catches, a hurried puff at a cigarette cupped in a careful hand, and then again the watchful stare up the deserted street, with the yellow glare of the street lamps making pools of light.

At last came the thing everyone had been waiting for – waiting, dreading, expecting. There was a sudden burst of automatic fire at close range, and on the edges of the pool of light 150 yards away dark figures could be seen dashing for the cover of a low wall.

Immediately one of the defenders sent a quick burst from his automatic at the nearest light, and instantly darkness fell. At the same time, others raked the street ahead with gunfire, while two hurled stick grenades in case the unseen attackers were still moving forward.

This was Beirut, capital city of the country once called the most civilized in the Middle East. And the battle ground was no distant suburb or little known slum quarter. This was the beginning of the battle of Kantari, the opening round of what became known as 'the fight for the hotels', a savage, bloody, desperate struggle for control of some of the tallest buildings in Beirut, a battle which was to go on for months.

It was on Saturday, 25 October 1975 that the battle for Kantari began. By that time the war in Lebanon had been going on for seven months, so the crump of exploding shells and rattle of machine-gun fire was nothing new to the tired people of the city. What was new was the sudden escalation of the fighting and the appearance of a new force. Up to now, the months of battle had been a static form of warfare in fixed places – the newspapers had already begun calling Ain Rumaneh and

Chiah, Hadeth, Dekwaneh, Tal Zaatar, Sinn el Fil and all the others 'the traditional fronts'. Kantari was not one of them. It was a rather expensive residential area lying between the city centre to the west, the newly built international hotels to the north, the commercial district to the east and poorer Moslem suburbs to the south. And it was from one of these that the attack was launched.

In Zarif, up the hill from Kantari, they had been preparing all day. Ibrahim Kleilat, leader of a little-known political group called the Independent Nasserites, was at his makeshift command post in the apartment of one of his followers from the early morning onwards. Mortars were set up in car parks near the Public Gardens, the one open space in crowded Beirut, where land had become gold over the past few booming years. His militiamen, the Mourabitoun, the 'Sentinels', quietly moved forward into the Sanayeh district, just one block away from a Lebanese Army barracks. The guards there carefully saw nothing and as night fell they retired into the cantonment, closing and barring the gate behind them. Only the Mourabitoun were on the streets, a few local people who had to get back to their own homes, and foreigners who had business there.

One of these foreigners was Phil Caputo, a correspondent of the Chicago *Daily News*. He had to go to the Reuter office in the Union National building in Sanayeh Square to file a dispatch and, when he reached there, he found armed men milling about the entrance. He showed them his Lebanese Press card, written in Arabic and French, and after careful scrutiny of this, Caputo was allowed in. He stayed there an hour or so, then left. The same man who had examined his pass on the way in was still at the door, but now it was another militiaman who was checking identities. He asked for the pass, Caputo produced it, but pointed to the other man and said he had already seen it and knew him. The new man on duty did not like being told what he should or should not do. Angrily he waved Caputo away. Then, when the American was fifty yards down the street, he casually raised his gun and opened fire. Caputo was hit. He fell down, then started crawling away. Again came a burst of fire, and again Caputo was hit. A tough ex-Marine Lieutenant, he managed to drag him-

12

self to comparative safety round the corner, and called for help to men sheltering in a garage. They would not risk going across the road to him, but beckoned him over. Laboriously, he crawled across, and was eventually picked up and taken by a roundabout route to the Trad Hospital in Rue Mexique. A few days later he had to be taken out of there in an armoured personnel carrier as that once-safe area became a battle ground.

Up in Sanayeh the Mourabitoun were forming up into their assault squads, and the mortarmen were trying a few ranging bombs. In spite of all the empty streets, eyes were everywhere, and each movement was quickly passed on to the Phalangist forward headquarters opposite the Starco building in Daouk Omar. It was these hastily whispered messages over the telephone which led to the furious activity in Kantari, the swift new barricades and the general alert among the quarter's Phalangist defenders. For although Kantari was what was known in Beirut as a 'mixed' area, a place where Moslems and Christians both lived, it was totally under the control of the powerful Right-wing Phalangist Party, and it was the Christian men of the district, party members to a man, who provided the first line of defence.

Usually, it was only the young men who stood on guard each night, checking passers-by if they were not known, smiling and saying a polite 'Bon soir' to known residents, 'arresting' strangers – usually Moslems or people found to be members of one of the opposition parties. Sometimes, the dozen or so men on duty needed quick help, and then a pre-arranged plan went into action. It had happened the previous evening. The Mourabitoun, preparing for their major offensive into Phalangist territory, sent half a dozen small squads of fighters on probing missions into the area, testing the defences, deliberately drawing fire to pin-point the position of the guards. So many sudden eruptions of activity in so many places was too much for the couple of dozen men on duty. Quickly the message was sent back by one of the dozen or so boys who went out each night with their elder brothers. The lad went running into a house in Rue Clemenceau and moments later a tall figure in a dark soutane hurried along the road to the darkened church of St Elie. A minute later the bells rang out

13

as the curé sounded the traditional Lebanese Christian call to arms. Instantly, doors opened in every street within hearing distance and middle-aged and elderly men emerged, rifles in their hands, bandoliers across their jackets and webbing belts with pouches of ammunition and grenades around their ample waists. With hardly a word to each other they hurried to their positions, waited a few minutes to let their eyes become accustomed to the darkness, then methodically and calmly began firing into the blackness.

Now, on the night of the main assault, everyone was already in position. They knew in advance that the attack was coming, and had made their preparations. What was still unsure was where the main thrust would come and, even as the battle started, it was still not clear what would be the main objective of the Mourabitoun attack, for at first it seemed no more than a general assault. From their forward positions in Sanayeh and their headquarters back in Zarif, the Mourabitoun moved down Avenue Spears, then turned left past the home of Takieddin Solh – Taki Bey, Prime Minister only months before – to try to shoot their way down Rue May Ziade, while another group took up their positions at the top of Rue Mexique and engaged the Phalangist defenders half-way down that narrow street.

But these two attacks, though eventually they were to lead to victory for the Mourabitoun in this phase of the battle, were no more than feints to disguise the true objective. The defenders should have realized this, for they knew its importance as well as their opponents. The Murr Tower was the tallest building in Beirut, and it was almost finished. It had only been started about a year before, but by a remarkable new process of pre-fabrication perfected by a Lebanese construction company, it was going up at the rate of a storey every few days, and now its thirty concrete floors were finished, and everything was ready for the plasterers and decorators and all the others who would finish off this massive new symbol of Christian dominance of the prosperous Lebanese service economy. The Murr Tower was owned by a prominent Phalangist supporter, Michel Murr. And by dint of generous contributions to Party funds and his influence with the Party hierarchy, Mr Murr had made sure that his new building would

14

not become involved in the battles going on all over Beirut. Of course, the Phalangists, in whose territory it was, were eager to make use of this wonderful vantage point. From its upper floors, they knew, their guns could dominate the Moslem areas to the south-east, and observation posts on the roof would ensure early warning of any attack. But Mr Murr would not let them go up his expensive new tower. The reason was simple: by the roundabout methods so easily employed in Beirut, the Palestinian Resistance Movement had sent Mr Murr a message. They told him that if the Phalangists were allowed to use the new building, then at some time in the future they would blow it up. Not immediately, perhaps, but when it was finally completed. And when it was occupied. At that comparatively early stage in the Lebanese war, people were still thinking that life would return to what they called 'normal' in a matter of months. So Mr Murr took the warning very seriously, and with his influence and money made sure that no Phalangist guns were placed on any of the floors of his tall new building.

Of course, the Phalangist militiamen realized the importance of the Tower, so a strong guard was left around its base, with machine guns carefully placed and strong points with good fields of fire established. Some fifteen men were there on that Saturday night, a more than adequate force to repel the kind of attack anticipated. But, as the sounds of battle grew all round, it was impossible for those young Phalangists, 'regulars' in Sheikh Pierre Gemayel's ten-thousand-strong militia, to sit quietly waiting for an attack they did not believe would ever come, while their comrades were in the thick of battle all round them. So off went ten of the fifteen guards to reinforce their hard-pressed friends only a few blocks away. And within minutes of their departure came the assault they had not believed would happen. Firing at any movement they saw, the Mourabitoun stormed in, hurling grenades, spraying automatic fire, making it impossible for the tiny band of defenders to hold out. The Phalangists retreated to the first floor and there they were able to hold off the attackers for an hour as two or three Mourabitoun at a time tried to storm up the unfinished concrete stairs. Outside the attackers were in firm control, and had established their ·50 calibre machine guns within lethal range. A steady stream of fire went in through the openings in the bare concrete where windows were supposed to be. Again the Phalangists had to retreat, though no-one knew how many there were by this time. Another hour and it was all over. The last Phalangist was killed still firing his rifle, still vainly trying to hold on to the building denied them by the concern for possible future advantage of one of their own supporters. Now the unknown Mourabitoun were in control of the Murr Tower, and soon showed the way they meant to use it – with none of the squeamishness of the previous Phalangist 'owners'.

A picked squad hurried up to the twenty-third floor and began setting up gun emplacements that covered both sides of the building. Sandbags were filled, the debris of the building operations pressed into service, and the heavy machine guns installed. Only an hour after their seizure of the building, the Mourabitoun began putting it to use. On one side a group of sharp-shooters picked off anyone moving in the Wadi abou Jamil, the main street of the Jewish Quarter of Beirut, which was being used by the Phalangists to move their reinforcements from their headquarters at Sioufi up to the hard-pressed Kantari area. On the other side the machine guns covered the intersections at the eastern end of Rue Clemenceau, so that the Phalangist militia moving in had to take a roundabout route up through the Holiday Inn, soon itself to become the centre of the bitterest fighting for the quarter.

This quick seizure of the Murr Tower was the main success of the night, for on all the other battle fronts the Phalange was able to repel the attacks. In Rue Mexique and May Ziade the defenders held their sandbagged positions because the Mourabitoun found it impossible to storm down these straight short streets in the face of the withering fire-power the defenders could muster. So, as another dawn broke to the steady sounds of battle, on the ground the position was much the same as it had been the night before, the only difference being that the upper end of Rue Hamra, the main artery of the city centre, and the eastern end of Rue Clemenceau were denied to the Phalangists – or indeed to anyone else, for at this early stage the Mourabitoun were totally indiscriminate in their targets. Their motto seemed to be: if it moves, shoot it. The result was that once again the centre of Beirut was deserted, and the couple of hundred people killed during the day as usual included a high proportion of civilians, old men or boys, people who had to go out of their homes in search of bread or other food or of water, for in many houses the water was already running short.

There were casualties as well among those who should not have been out at all. In blind adherence to habit or out of some strange loyalty to their jobs, many of the small traders on whom Beirut so largely depended still tried to go about their business. Hussein Farawaz, the newsagent on Rue Fakhreddine, at the bottom of the same street in which the Murr Tower stood, had been sleeping in his tiny hole-in-the-wall shop and, when none of his newspaper wholesalers delivered his bundles of papers, he got out his moped and set off to collect them himself. Then he calmly began delivering them, doing a roaring trade with the Phalangists still crouched behind their barricades at each street corner. Twice Farawaz was pinned down by gunfire, but still he went on. Only when he got back to his little shop did he realize how foolhardy he had been. His small son was there to tell him that his brother had been shot through the stomach on his way to 'rescue' Hussein. Father and son got on the moped and set off for their home, never again to try to deliver newspapers in the heart of a combat zone.

As attackers and defenders settled down to a day of desultory exchanges of fire in a pattern that was to become familiar over the months – reserving the nights for the real attempts to take territory or score victories – a huge pall of smoke hung over the commercial district of the city, a mile to the east. This was the area of warehouses, banks, airline offices, the Bourse, all the myriad facets of the service economy on which Beirut depended. It was the area, too, of the *souks*, the labyrinth of narrow streets each housing all the practitioners of the same trade. There was the vegetable *souk*, the clothes *souk*, the meat *souk* and so on. Above all, there was the gold *souk*, two glittering streets where every shop front was a treasure house of bangles and rings, chains, lockets and precious stones. Many of the gold dealers were Armenians, there were a few Jews, and some Maronites, the dominant Christian group whose militant organization was the Phalangist Party. In the other *souks*,

17

Moslems and Christians traded side by side, though as usual the poorer majority, the old clothes dealers and so on, were usually Moslems. But whatever the religion of the stall-holders and shop-keepers, everyone recognized that the *souks* played a major part in the economic life of the city. Local people did all their shopping there, it was a regular attraction for tourists, and the traders imported and exported as well as carrying on their retail business. By any standards, the *souks* of Beirut belonged to everyone and were of benefit to everyone. Yet for days the Phalangists had been pouring in mortars and rockets, raking the shops with heavy machine-gun fire from their positions only a hundred or so yards away, and doing everything they could to destroy the area. It seemed senseless, though in fact it was part of the general Phalangist strategy. Their aim in Beirut was not only the classic military concept of destroying the enemy – the Left-wing forces and the Palestinians – it was also to involve as many people on their side as possible. In particular, the Phalangists wanted the Army brought into the fighting. The Lebanese Army, a mere eighteen thousand strong, was still the most powerful force in the country, with tanks, armoured cars, personnel carriers, artillery and all the other equipment any modern army must have. It was the one properly organized group, with a command structure, good communications, adequate reserves of ammunition, and men who were well-trained and obedient. From the Phalangist point of view, the Army also had one other great recommendation: it was commanded by a Maronite of known Phalangist sympathies and the majority of the officers were Maronites. The Phalangist calculation was plain, though it was never spelt out. If the Army could be embroiled, then no matter how much its neutrality was proclaimed, or even if the Command did actually try to remain impartial, inevitably the troops would be forced to fight on the side of the Phalangist militia – the experience of half a dozen different clashes in the past had shown that this was always the case.

But it was not only the Phalangists who realized that the Army's loyalty was suspect. So too did the Government headed by Rashid Karami, the Sunni Moslem Prime Minister. And he had set his face firmly against any involvement of the military. At the end of the 1958 civil war, only two institutions of the State had emerged unscathed and had formed the basis on which the country had been able to build anew: the Presidency and the Army. In this new civil war, the institution of the Presidency was already being damaged by the obvious partisanship of the President himself, Suleiman Franjieh. Mr Karami calculated that only by keeping the Army out of the conflict was there a faint hope of preserving some form of order on which to build in the future. The Prime Minister knew, too, that if he did unleash the Army in Beirut he would be accused by all Moslems in the country of siding with the Right, and would lose what influence he still had. On these two counts Karami was determined that the Army should stay out; so, despite the pleas of the Right-wing members of his own cabinet, led by Camille Chamoun, the Minister of the Interior, and the wanton destruction being spread by the Phalange, Karami held out against the pressures and refused to give the orders which would have permitted the Army to move.

The destruction of the *souks* went on, with fires smouldering by day and new salvoes of mortar bombs and rockets crashing in by night. The hard-pressed Beirut fire brigade tried to put out the worst blazes, but the frequently heroic firemen could do little. Often they could get nowhere near the fires because of constant sniper fire, deliberately aimed at them by one side or the other to ensure the destruction of some particular place. There was the beginning, too, of the division of the city which was soon to become complete, and the discrimination based on the religion of a man shown on his identity card. Driving along Avenue Fuad Chehab, a fire engine was stopped by a Phalangist road block as it rushed to a fire, siren wailing. The Phalangists carefully examined the I.D. cards of the fire crew, then announced that only the Christian members of the team would be allowed through. With considerable courage, the Christian firemen then told their co-religionists that it was the whole crew or nothing. Both sides held their ground, and the fire engine and the men turned back, leaving another blaze to burn unchecked.

So bad was the situation that Damascus was asked to help – the first direct involvement of Syria in the Lebanese war, a humanitarian involvement very different from the one which was to come a few months later. Syrian fire engines and crews were sent from Damascus, and they too came under fire as they tried to help their Lebanese colleagues. So all over the commercial district and in the port, the fires raged unchecked as both sides joined in the orgy of destruction started in this particular case by the Phalangists, as they tried to pursue their strategic aim, through a deliberate scorched earth policy which probably caused as much damage to their own supporters and members as it did to the property of their opponents.

But one *souk* could not be allowed to go. Somehow, the gold *souk* had to be saved and on both sides of the line the powerful men who owned the shops were applying pressure. It was a demonstration of another facet of the Lebanese situation – the polarization of rich and poor, for in this war it was not only Moslem against Christian, Palestinian against Phalangist, it was also rich versus poor, haves against have nots, Shia Moslem against Sunni Moslem. And now, Moslem and Christian owners of shops in the gold *souks* joined with Jews and Armenians to plead with both sides to save their capital and their livelihood. Their powerful collective voice was listened to with respect, and soon a commando group of the Lebanese Army, one-hundred-and-fifty-strong, was on its way to the *souk* under a promise of safe conduct and no molestation from either side. The soldiers got there just in time, for others, too, had heard of the plans to clear the treasure from the *souk*. As the soldiers were hurrying by back ways to the entrance to the *souk* at the top of the Place des Martyrs, a fifty-strong band of gangsters had shot their way in, killing the few guards still on duty and braving the fire of the Phalange on one side of the square and the Leftists on the other. While most of the robbers took up positions ready to hold off anyone who tried to interfere, others tore off the shutters of the shops or blasted their way in with dynamite. They were hastily filling sacks with gold ornaments as the Army arrived. And in this first engagement it was the Army which quickly came off best. The soldiers, with their armoured vehicles, could go right up to the entrance to the *souk* with impunity as they poured in machine-gun and cannon fire. Within minutes those thieves who were not killed had fled, and the Army had scored a notable victory in a dubious cause.

Under the protection of the guns of the military, the waiting merchants arrived to load their treasure into cars and trucks. Many of them were unwilling to take such a tempting cargo far, so they did no more than drive half a mile to the main office of the British Bank of the Middle East in Bab Idriss. There they hastily packed their gold into the strong-boxes that they had previously rented, then went on their way carrying only a few items they thought they might be able to sell in the makeshift *souks* which were beginning to appear in other parts of the city.

As the merchants were getting their capital out of a danger area, in the streets around Kantari those people who could were leaving. Hundreds of foreigners lived in the district and for many of them it was their first close experience of the war which had sounded as distant thunder or the occasional burst of rifle fire. Dozens of them managed to get out during that first weekend, often braving bursts from automatics as they drove heavily loaded cars fast up wrong-way streets to avoid the gunmen. Others were forced by the intensity of the crossfire to stay in their apartments, and for them it was the beginning of a week or ten days of constant bombardment, a period of living in cellars, scratching an existence from the stores of tinned food everyone had laid in, and spending the days listening to the radio to find out what was happening just outside their own doors, for in most places it was too dangerous even to look over a balcony.

Few of the Lebanese residents of the area were able to move. They had nowhere to go and they knew better than most that, if they did abandon their homes, at the first lull gangs of looters would descend on them, and nothing would be left. What was not expected was the wanton destruction that took place for no reason but that an owner was of the 'wrong' religion. At the top of Rue Mexique, for instance, stood a small *pension* run by Hans Matchek, an Arabic-speaking Austrian who had lived and worked in Iraq and Lebanon most of his life. Early on the morning of the first Mourabitoun attack on Kantari, Kleilat's men walked into the place as the staff and the few residents still there were having their breakfast. The raiders took most of the staff prisoner, then sprayed petrol all over the premises and set it alight. Within an hour, the once neat and orderly Austrian *pension* was a burnt-out smouldering shell.

The owner, Matchek, was to spend the next fortnight with his wife and two sons in the basement of his apartment building in the next street, as that too suddenly became the centre of a raging battle.

Over in Achrafiyah, the middle-class Christian suburb which was one of the strongholds of the Phalangist Party, the people were not having an easy time either. Night after night they huddled in basements or stairwells as the mortars pounded in and the rockets burst through walls. One group of hardy Phalangists went up on to the roof of a building with shotguns and put up a barrage of pellets whenever they heard a rocket swishing overhead. In a surprising number of cases they managed to hit the rockets, which exploded in mid-air at the slightest impact. The missiles being used were comparatively slow-moving, and any contact was enough to set them off. Other people were less bold. Crouching with his family near the lift shaft of his building, Akram Hannouche noticed that one of his neighbours seemed totally unconcerned about the constant pounding the building was taking. Hannouche discovered the reason when his friend offered to share a drink with him. It was *arak*, the strong Lebanese-made anisette which turns from colourless to milky white when water is added. But instead of topping his drink up with water, this embattled resident was using vodka. One glass and the worst barrage seemed insignificant.

A week after it began, the battle for Kantari ended. And it ended as bloodily as it had gone on all the time. The Mourabitoun had been inching forward in Rue Mexique, Rue May Ziade, along Rue Clemenceau and through the backyards and lanes. In the afternoon, they made their final assault. A savage mortar bombardment was followed by intense machine-gun fire, then the assault squads moved forward. In some places the defenders stood and fought at point-blank range, for the quarter was no longer being defended by the ill-trained young men who lived there. Early on in the battle a group of some fifty tough Phalangist militiamen had been brought in, full-time members not only of the Party but also of its 'army', men who had fought against the Palestinians in the clashes which had taken place every year since 1969. The battle-hardened veterans died where they stood, hurling grenades and even

22

using pistols as the Mourabitoun overran their positions. The sheer weight of numbers of the attackers and the fire-power they could deploy were too much for the defence. One by one the three-hundred-strong assault force took the machine-gun emplacements and strong-points, winkled snipers out of tall apartments and blasted defended positions with the lethally destructive recoilless rifles which were a new factor on the Beirut battlefield. Then, in the last stages of their mopping-up operation, as they stormed the final approach to the Phalangist-held Holiday Inn, the Mourabitoun went through the houses in the short street called Emir Omar. If they found a young man, he was shot. If they found an old man wearing what looked like part of a military uniform, he was shot. If they found a girl wearing khaki trousers, she was shot. Altogether, some forty people were killed in Rue Emir Omar that afternoon – not a high total by the awful standards which the Lebanese war was to establish, but high enough. And because the whole operation was basically a minor affair, a peripheral battle, there were few who knew what went on, and fewer still who cared.

With Kantari in their hands, the Mourabitoun set about looting in another pattern which was to become familiar over the months and years. Even as some of the fighters were winkling out the last sniper from a building in Rue Clemenceau, others were breaking in apartment doors and carrying off everything movable. Soon trucks began arriving to take away the bulkier objects – Persian carpets, tapestries, expensive furniture. In this area it all had to be done quickly and at some risk, for the Holiday Inn, an ugly twenty-six-storey slab completed only a year before, was still held by the Phalangists and they, like the Mourabitoun in the Murr Tower less than a mile away, fired at anything that moved in their field of vision. But the hotel was beleaguered by now: above it in Kantari the Mourabitoun were firmly in control and night after night they poured in fire until the neat blue and white façade of the building became a shell-pocked, smoke-blackened monument to the waste and futility of war. To the north-west, the attackers had moved into Phoenicia Street, once the centre of Beirut's night-life, with girlie bars, restaurants and gaudy hotels. The Palm Beach and the Excelsior Hotels were turned into strong-points, and at one time were trading fire with St Georges Hotel just across the way – Beirut's most prestigious and best-known hotel – now occupied by a party of Phalangists desperately trying to keep a supply route open to their hard-pressed comrades in the Holiday Inn.

After their quick success in Kantari, the Mourabitoun seemed to run out of steam. This was the first appearance of the Independent Nasserite Party's militia in the streets, and they had fought tenaciously and well to prove themselves a match for any of the other proliferating private armies. Trained in secret in small groups, financed and supplied by Libya, they had demonstrated that they were a new and powerful force in the complicated Lebanese equation, a force that would have to be taken into account in the future. Having made their point, they were content to sit back for a while, to collect the spoils of war and leave it to their leaders to reap the political harvest. And Ibrahim Kleilat, little more than a local gangster – an *abadiyah*, or district gun-boss, in the Lebanese argot – was doing very well in that task. Soon he became a regular member of the Left-wing and Palestinian conclaves which were held almost daily to decide on new moves or to counter Rightist efforts. Just as the success of his men in combat meant his voice was listened to in the councils of the Left, so the process led to further gains. More men joined his colours as his fame spread, and the additional men meant more clout for Kleilat in the council chambers. From being a local thug, Kleilat was rapidly being transformed into a politician – a standard process which had happened often in the past in Lebanon.

The battle of Kantari, brief but bloody, was a turning point in the Lebanese War because it extended the area of combat, involved foreigners and thus ensured international publicity, and changed the war from static exchanges of fire to real efforts to seize and hold territory. It was a totally new departure in a war that was already seven months old, a war which started with a political dispute and was deliberately fanned by a cold-blooded massacre.

2

Prelude to a war

The possibility of a war between Right-wing Lebanese parties and the Palestinians had existed ever since the commandoes emerged as a force in 1969. Year after year there had been clashes between the Palestine Resistance Movement and the Phalangists, often with the Lebanese Army becoming involved, but always the government of the day had managed to smooth things over, often at the last moment and at the cost of some surrender of Lebanese sovereignty. On each occasion, the price was thought worth paying, for everyone realized that if a full-scale clash did develop then it could easily spread to involve the whole country. The politicians and the man in the street alike knew that if a commando-Phalangist battle was allowed to go unchecked then very soon everyone else would be drawn in, the country would be split, and the civil war which everyone dreaded would begin. So in the past the politicians, the party leaders and the Palestinians had always managed to pull back from the brink. In 1975 the position was different. No longer were the Palestinians on their own, capable of calling on the support of the Moslem masses only after some incident had made it necessary. Now the situation was reversed. It was the poor Moslem section of the community which was making the running and involving the Palestinians on their side, rather than the other way around as it always had been in the past. It was Israel which was largely responsible for the change in the state of affairs. It has always been Israeli policy to retaliate strongly whenever the Palestinian commandoes undertook an operation – the usual forms of revenge were aerial bombardment of places always described as 'terrorist bases' in Lebanon, or ground operations by Israeli troops who crossed the border into Lebanon to

25

search out and destroy houses said to be used as starting places for guerrilla attacks or to take prisoners. The usual targets for the Israeli cross-border raids were the villages of southern Lebanon lying on the road which ran parallel to the border between the two countries, mainly small communities of Shia Moslem farmers, who made a not very good living by growing crops of indifferent tobacco, which was bought at less-than-generous prices by the State Monopoly organization. The Shia of South Lebanon were amongst the poorest people in the country, a section which felt neglected by the Government in far-off Beirut and was bitter at the total lack of protection which allowed the Israeli forces to move at will in the border areas. In the past the people of the South had been able to do little but stage an occasional protest demonstration, often put down forcibly by the Internal Security Forces which were so notably absent whenever the Israelis made a raid. Their representatives in Parliament, led by Kamal Assad, the Speaker, visited them only when votes were needed. They were short of money, lacked schools, clinics or doctors, and felt themselves to be, as indeed they were, a community abandoned and ignored by the Central Government.

Then came a new development in Lebanon – the emergence of a powerful figure, a man whose voice was respected and listened to in the highest places in the land, a man who spoke up for the Shia when they could not speak for themselves. This new force on the political scene was the Imam Moussa Sad'r, a Persian of Lebanese origin, who returned to his ancestral home when in his thirties and rapidly established himself as a political figure as well as the head of his sect. The Imam's political aims were never in doubt and worried the conservatives among the Moslem leadership, who saw him as a rallying point for the younger, more articulate and naturally more radical members of their community. These serious misgivings came to a head in 1969, when the Imam proposed to establish a Shi'ite Moslem Higher Council to direct the affairs of the community, rather than leaving it to the Higher Moslem Council as in the past. This body, which spoke for all the Moslem religious sects, the Sunni and Druze as well as the Shia, was dominated by the old-guard politicians of the Sunni Moslem establishment – elderly men who had grown up with the State, who saw no need for any changes or innovations. By breaking away from this conservative body, Moussa Sad'r furthered his own political aims by giving himself a recognizable and powerful base, and he provided the discontented younger members of the Shia sect with a rallying point, and a strong voice which had to be heeded by the powerful and rich. To underline the point, Moussa Sad'r called a strike of all his followers in Beirut soon after he had taken over as head of the Shia Moslem Higher Council. The ostensible reason for the stoppage was to protest at the lack of protection for the villagers of the South against the constant Israeli incursions, but the real aim was to demonstrate Moussa Sad'r's power and to show the strength of the Shia community in the capital. In the past, it had always been held that the Christian Maronites were the largest single religious group in Lebanon, and that the Sunnis formed the bulk of the Moslem population. By the late 1960s everyone knew that this was no longer so, though the authorities were unwilling publicly to concede the point. The Imam's parade of his authority in Beirut, which was not a Shia stronghold, was intended to remind the Government of the facts, as well as to enhance his own political standing. This was made plain by the strikers' demand for greater protection for the South of the country, though the Imam knew as well as anyone that the Government in Beirut could not defend the villages along the border without transforming the country into one of the 'confrontation' states around Israel – a move which would have prompted an immediate pre-emptive strike by the Israelis and would have led to the end of Lebanon's very special position in the Middle East. The more realistic politicians in the country rightly proclaimed that 'our weakness is our strength', accurately reasoning that a near-defenceless posture would make it internationally impossible for Israel to move against Lebanon in any determined way or to annex any part of it, and counting the occasional raids against Palestine refugee camps or border villages as a small price to pay for the reasonable security which allowed the country to carry on its profitable role as middleman and financial centre of the Arab world.

In Israel, there was a very clear understanding of what was going on in Lebanon, and the professionals of the Ministry of Foreign Affairs quickly saw how the situation could be exploited. By continuing their raids into Lebanon they would fan the disaffection felt by the Shia of the south, and would thus help to polarize the factions in the country. This policy would contribute to the ultimate Israeli aim of moving by proxy against the Palestinians in Lebanon, and would also go some way towards countering the Palestinian argument which used Lebanon as the prime example of a state in which different communities and religions could live side by side. So the raids went on and the people of the South became increasingly embittered, though there is little doubt that on occasion they were encouraged to show their feelings by discreet promptings from Moussa Sad'r and his lieutenants. Sad'r had openly entered the political field by backing opponents of Kamal Assad, the traditional leader, in the parliamentary elections of 1972 and he was determined to whittle away the support of what he considered 'the Shia Right'. Constant agitation was one way of doing this, for Assad and his followers were identified with the régime of President Franjieh, and they could be made to share the blame for the total lack of security in the South. So, true to form, Israel kept up its raids on the frontier villages. There was one on the first day of 1975, and throughout the month the pressure was maintained as Israeli forces crossed into Lebanon and blew up bridges and roads 'to restrict Palestinian movements'. Of course, the Palestinians, travelling singly or a few at a time with nothing but their personal weapons or a rocket launcher, were hampered not at all; the ones who suffered, as the Israelis must have calculated, were the farmers trying to move their tobacco crops to the Régie in Nabatiyeh. Then came a concentrated Israeli artillery attack on the village of Kfar Chouba on the edge of what was known as 'Fatahland', the Arkoub area of South-East Lebanon where the Palestinians were given virtual freedom of action by the Cairo Agreement of 1969 which ended one of the earlier confrontations between the Resistance Movement and the Lebanese Army. The choice of Kfar Chouba was made, according to the Israelis, because it was used by Palestinians to launch raids across the border. This may well have been true, for practically every village on the frontier was used for this purpose, with the exception only of the two or three

28

Christian enclaves there. Kfar Chouba was useful for another reason: it presented a perfect artillery target, high on a hill and very close to the border, and it was within a few miles of Marjayoun, one of the main towns of the South and the headquarters of the Lebanese Army in the area. From Marjayoun it was possible to see the shells landing in the village, the simple stone-built houses crumbling, and the people fleeing with their meagre possessions. It was also possible to see the determined lack of any action by the Lebanese Army, whose role seemed to be merely to seal off the roads to Kfar Chouba and to direct the fleeing villagers to emergency centres belatedly set up once the Lebanese newspapers had reported the situation. Most of the villagers were quartered in schools and other buildings in Marjayoun, and they congregated each day in the main square to watch with stricken eyes their homes being systematically pounded. Eventually, they began demonstrating against the lack of help they were receiving, and then the Army was able to move, firing shots in the air and dispersing the hapless villagers with rifle butts. Soon many of them made their way to Beirut, a procession of hopeless and bitter people which even the politicians could not ignore.

First to take any public stand on the matter was Sheikh Pierre Gemayel, leader of the Phalangist Party, though he said nothing about helping the villagers or protecting the South. His line was that the causes of Israeli action should be removed. The Israelis only attacked in response to provocations from the Palestinians, he said: 'The time has come to reassert Lebanese authority over the border areas.' This was, of course, just what Israel wanted, for if it was to re-establish its control over the South, the Lebanese State would be brought into direct confrontation with the Palestinians, a development which was always the ultimate though unacknowledged aim of Israeli policy.

Yasser Arafat, the head of the Palestine Liberation Organization and leader of el Fatah, the main guerrilla group, understood the situation as well as anyone else and did his best to avoid the trap. Instead of speaking in tough terms about the Cairo Agreement or about the rights 'given' to the commandoes, he took a conciliatory attitude to Gemayel's provocative statement, promised to put all the Palestinians' 'meagre resources' at the service of Lebanon, and was suitably humble and grateful for the 'hospitality' which the Palestinians had received.

Once again a crisis was averted and the lid put on an affair which had threatened to get out of hand. A few weeks later the Arab League meeting in Cairo voted to give Lebanon £36 million to help with the 'reconstruction' of the South, and the refugees who had emigrated to Beirut were absorbed into 'the poverty belt' surrounding the capital, invisible as an organized force among all the others who clung to a precarious existence within sight of the high-rise apartment blocks and the offices of the wealthy.

These demonstrations by the Shia in the South and the way in which Lebanese citizens had begun to make the running should have been a warning to the establishment in Beirut. Yet they refused to see the writing on the wall and made no attempt to alleviate the situation. A few pounds of the aid voted by the Arab states did begin to trickle down to the poor, though most of it stuck to the fingers of the politicians and their cronies who were supposed to distribute it. And life in Beirut went on, with the pursuit of more and more money and more and more power as the main consideration. Beirut at this stage was still regarded by other Arab states as a fruitful site for investment and Saudi Arabian, Kuwaiti and other financiers were constantly on the look-out for opportunities to buy land and erect new apartment blocks or hotels, to buy their way into established companies, or to take shares in the fifty or so foreign banks established in the country. From past experience, these investors were well aware of one fact of life: to succeed in business in Lebanon it was essential to have a Lebanese partner and preferably one with a good deal of influence of his own. Thus a group of Kuwaiti businessmen who planned to set up a modern fishing industry in Lebanese waters thought they had scored a considerable success when they persuaded Camille Chamoun to be chairman of Proteine Ltd, the trawler-owning and fish-processing firm into which they had put their money. Unfortunately, as is usual with private Kuwaiti enterprises, in contrast to the carefully researched way in which the Government of that state invested its money, the backers of the scheme had done nothing to find out the local situation. They had reports of adequate shoals of fish some distance off shore, they had technical studies setting out the type of boats and equipment needed, but they had done nothing to see how their new enterprise would affect the Lebanese people most closely concerned or what repercussions there might be. They were to learn the hard way. The fishermen of Tyre and Sidon had heard only the sketchiest rumours of what was planned, and all they could find in their newspapers were reports of the large investment which was to be made, descriptions of the fast and powerful modern trawlers which were to be bought, and references to the personal interest of Mr Chamoun, one of the more extreme Christian leaders, who was less than popular in the Moslem, rather Left-wing towns of Tyre and Sidon. So, egged on by the agitators always hovering on the fringes of political life, the fishermen took to the streets. They looked at the open boats they were using, locally built and powered only by a simple outboard engine, and contrasted them with the pictures of the new trawlers they saw in the papers. They talked among themselves of the diminishing catches they were getting – carefully ignoring the fact that the decimation of the shoals was largely their own work, due to their habit of fishing by throwing sticks of dynamite into the water, a process which destroyed fish of every size. They discussed the difficulties they had in trying to get loans to buy new nets or engines and the poor prices they got for their catches. And again they looked at the reports of what was to happen in the paper, and recalled the role played by Camille Chamoun when he was President in 1958 and the actions of the National Liberal Party ever since.

So the fishermen's demonstrations began, a genuinely popular movement with a real grievance in spite of the fact that it was based on incomplete knowledge and partial reporting – the Proteine company planned to fish far off shore and would have been unlikely to do much damage to the type of inshore fishing practised by the local people. Marches were organized, and then came that peculiarly Lebanese form of protest, the spreading of burning tyres across roads to make them impassable to traffic. On this occasion it was the main North–South coastal highway which was blocked, a road which carried a great deal of traffic every day and which was vital for taking the agricultural produce of the South to Beirut to keep the hungry city fed. Huge queues of cars backed up, and in Beirut expected deliveries were not made. It was a situation which caused a great deal of annoyance to the powerful merchants and businessmen whose support was important to the Government. And the fishermen themselves were a poor lot, few in number and with minimal power. It seemed a perfect opportunity for the weak Government of Rashid Solh to show that it could indeed act decisively when necessary.

There was an urgent need for Solh to do so. Ever since he had been installed as Prime Minister in the autumn of 1974 – a compromise Government leader chosen by the President more to further certain political ends than to govern the country – there had been a steady deterioration in the security situation in Lebanon. Blood feuds which had lain dormant for generations were revived in the primitive Akkar region of the North, robberies and violence were the order of the day in every town and city, corruption was so blatant that it was at last becoming a public scandal, and the police and security forces stood idly by, apparently unable or unwilling to exercise the authority of the State. Even Rashid Solh, a backbench Deputy who was not part of the Sunni Moslem establishment and therefore not real Prime-Ministerial material, realized that something had to be done. Yet so many were his political debts, and so circumscribed his actions if he was not to offend those who had put him in power and were for the moment keeping him there, that he had to be extremely careful what targets he chose. A few weeks before, he had successfully moved against a notorious outlaw, Ahmed Kaddour, a man of huge personality and personal bravery, who had chosen to put his considerable talents to work on the wrong side of the law. Kaddour was a murderer several times over, a robber and a brigand. By force of arms he and a small band of gangsters had taken over most of the old town of Tripoli, making their headquarters in the centuries-old buildings at the heart of the labyrinth of narrow streets which made up the *souks* there, exacting tribute from the small merchants and traders, and offering refuge to any gangster on the run who was willing to use his gun on their behalf. The respectable townspeople of Tripoli were cut off from a considerable area of their own city

32

and were constantly at risk from the depradations of the outlaws in their midst. For these reasons, and perhaps also to
demonstrate that Rashid Karami, his political enemy and the
feudal master of Tripoli, was unable to do anything, Rashid
Solh did at last send strong detachments of the security forces
to root out the gangsters. They succeeded very well and,
emboldened by this success, Solh determined to use an equally
firm hand to halt the unrest around Sidon. He dispatched
detachments of the security forces to the South and even had
Army units standing by. At first all was well. The security men
cleared the roads and got the traffic moving again, but they
could not remove the causes of the trouble, and on 26 February
a massive protest march was held in Sidon. At the head of the
procession as it wound through the town was Maarouf Sa'ad,
the local mayor and a former Deputy, a white-haired, smiling,
rubicund man who backed the Nasserite movement and accurately reflected the mood of his people in a way few Lebanese
leaders managed to do.

No permission to hold the march had been sought, though
officially all such demonstrations needed Government
approval in advance. In a country where such utter lawlessness
prevailed, it was hardly surprising that Maarouf Sa'ad and his
supporters had dispensed with this requirement. So, when the
long procession of marchers, carrying banners and shouting
slogans, turned on to the main road in Sidon, the small group
of Lebanese Internal Security men, under the command of a
lieutenant, had every legal right to stop them. What happened
next, however, was not what the Government or anyone else
would have wished. The young lieutenant, disconcerted by the
approach of such a huge group of people, was clearly at a loss
about what to do, and the sight of a locally powerful man in
the front rank could have made it no easier for him. Obviously
the marchers were not going to be deterred by orders from
a tiny group of gendarmerie and a very junior officer, so the
young lieutenant ordered his men to fire in the air to warn
the demonstrators to stop. Somehow, a bullet from that volley
in the air managed to hit Maarouf Sa'ad – though later
Government and Army apologists were to claim that it was
someone not involved in the confrontation, some mysterious
agent provocateur, who had fired the fatal shot. For it did prove

33

fatal, in more ways than one. Maarouf Sa'ad was rushed to hospital, where he died from the wound he had received after a week of desperate efforts to save his life. The shot was also to provide the *coup de grâce* for the tottering Government of Rashid Solh, as well as to mark the beginning of the Lebanese civil war.

Certainly this new show of firmness by the Government was totally counter-productive. Heavy fighting broke out all over Sidon at the beginning of March, with two soldiers killed on the first day, as Army reinforcements were rushed in, and five more the next day. In the usual reaction of weak régimes trying to be strong, Rashid Solh's Government refused to acknowledge that it had made an error in seeking to take a tough stand against the Sidon fishermen and their sympathizers, and instead of seeking some face-saving formula it tried to continue its heavy-handed approach. Further reinforcements were dispatched and so were lorry loads of gendarmerie and some regular Army units with armoured cars and personnel carriers, but just as the Syrians were to find Sidon a tough nut to crack a year later so, too, the Lebanese Army found it had bitten off more than it could chew. The reason, of course, was that it was not a group of poor fishermen and their supporters that the Army had to deal with, but the well-organized and heavily-armed southern command of the Palestine Resistance Movement, which had come to the aid of its friends. In the past, it had been the other way about, with the Moslem Left supporting the Palestinians. Now, the debt was being repaid.

The Army could make little headway against the determined resistance it met in Sidon. One attack was repulsed with some loss, while the Army column on the main road just north of the town found itself out-flanked by commandoes who seized and held the high ground to the east and made any exposed section of the road a hazard. Force did not seem to be the answer to the problem, but under orders from the Army Commander, General Iskander Ghanem, light field artillery guns were moved into position and the Army began a desultory shelling of buildings in Sidon said to be strong-points used by the Palestinians. Not for the first or last time, the Lebanese Army was being used to reduce one of their own country's main towns.

Eventually, some sanity was restored to the situation. Khaled Jumblatt, the Minister of Economy in Rashid Solh's Cabinet and a leading member of the Progressive Socialist Party founded by his name-sake Kamal Jumblatt, went to the outskirts of Sidon to watch the Army attempt to move in. The Colonel in charge pointed out that, if the troops were ordered in, they would be sure to suffer heavy losses and, if they did get into the town, there was little they could do, as there were no strictly military objectives for them to take. Equally, said this sensible and articulate officer, if the bombardment of the town was to continue, there would certainly be heavy casualties among the townspeople and, again, the likelihood of any useful result was minimal. Mr Jumblatt agreed and by roundabout means sent a message to Abou Zaim, commander of the Palestinians in southern Lebanon. Abou Zaim, a stocky, middle-aged man who had distinguished himself in earlier fighting with the Lebanese Army rather than with the Israeli enemy, was by now more concerned with a quiet life than with military glory. He was all in favour of arranging a truce, but wisely referred the matter to the Palestinian command. They, too, agreed that a negotiated settlement of this imbroglio was needed and sent one of their more experienced men to the South to arrange matters. Hassan Salameh, known as Abou Hassan in accordance with the Palestinian custom of using *noms de guerre*, had started in the movement as Arafat's body-guard, but his ready intelligence and undoubted bravery marked him for promotion. According to the Israelis, he was closely involved in directing the activities of Black September, the extremist organization responsible for acts of terrorism and murder all over the world, though there was little evidence of this. Abou Hassan's title was Chief of Security and it was in this capacity that he negotiated with the representatives of the Government. A ceasefire was agreed in return for the with-drawal of the Army, the promise of no victimization of those involved, and an undertaking to examine the fishermen's griev-ances which had sparked off the whole affair. Having settled these points, Abou Zaim and Abou Hassan, with two guards and a driver, set off along the lonely road in a small car from the forward Army positions into the heart of Sidon. The Army units on the edge of the town had been told by radio not to open fire, but it was thought doubtful that the Palestinians could be restrained in a similar way. This was an underestimate of the commando organization. In fact, their communications were almost as good as those of the Army in this sector and the fighters on the ground in Sidon were kept in touch with what was going on. Within minutes of the two commando leaders arriving in Sidon, the guns fell silent in a display of efficiency and discipline which neither the Army nor the Government representatives present had expected and which was not lost on them.

This opening skirmish of the civil war left a total of twenty-four dead, and it also led to a reassessment of the position of the Palestinians by that small group of people in the Government still concerned with such matters and not occupied solely with some factional interest, for the Sidon events had shown the Palestinians in a new light: they had proved they were ready to help the Lebanese Left and the largely Moslem section of the poorest stratum of society in disputes which had nothing at all to do with the Palestinian movement as such. They had shown, too, that they were quite pepared to take on the Lebanese Army and that they were able to give a very good account of themselves in such an encounter. The Army Command and the more responsible Civil Servants must have realized that they had been given an insight into changed conditions, but the Phalangist Party showed no such understanding, for the Sidon events, which ended in a truce and a compromise as usual, left a residue of bitterness which the Right-wing was quick to seize upon. The actions of the Army in shelling the town were condemned by all the Left, the Palestinians, and the Moslem leaders. In contrast, on the Right there were ostentatious demonstrations of support for the Army, which may have started spontaneously, but very soon became part of the Phalangist strategy. For weeks any Army ceremony, passing-out parade or even some routine guard-mounting exercise became the opportunity for the Phalangists to put on a noisy show of solidarity. The object, of course, was not only to assure the Army of Phalangist backing but also to seek to involve the Army on the side of the Right-wingers, and to identify the Army and the Phalangists in the minds of most people. It was a ploy which worked, though it did back-fire to some extent as the idea of Army–Phalangist duality became so embedded that Rashid Karami, when he became Prime Minister, resolutely refused to use the military to restore order in situations where he might have done so with some success if it had not been for this carefully nurtured idea that the Army was always on the side of the Phalangists.

It was the Phalangist Party which was making all the running now, though it was the Palestinians who had put on a show of muscle in Sidon. The Army had got the message, though somehow it had not registered with the Phalangists; it may have been that they interpreted the conciliatory statements by the Palestinian leaders after the fishermen's dispute as an admission of weakness. Whatever the reason, the Phalangists were obviously spoiling for trouble, and on Sunday 13 April they found their opportunity. The confrontation arose because both the Phalangists and the Palestinians were holding ceremonies on this day. On the Phalangist side, Sheikh Pierre Gemayel and a number of leaders of the party were at the dedication of a new church in Gemayel Street on the edge of the Christian suburb of Ain Rumaneh, an occasion which naturally called for strict security and vigilance by the Phalangist guards. On the Palestinian side, a rally was being held in Corniche Mazraa to mark the first anniversary of the Palestinian commando raid on the Israeli village of Kyriat Shmoneh, a raid which launched the series of suicide missions into Israel from Lebanon which had been a feature of the previous twelve months.

Naturally, there were different versions of what happened, but according to the evidence of the few impartial observers there were – Lebanese police and security men, though their testimony was bound to be suspect as they would be known for certain sympathies before being put on duty in a Christian area – according to these officers, the trouble began when a car carrying two commandoes was stopped at a Phalangist road block because its number plate was obscured, a fairly routine precaution by the Palestinians. An argument developed and, as usual, guns were produced and a shot was fired. One of the commandoes was wounded and was driven away by his comrade. Shortly afterwards, another car drove up to the street in which the Phalangist ceremony was taking place. It crashed through a road block and as soon as it came within range of a group of Phalangists, the commandoes in the car opened fire. Joseph Abu Assi, one of Gemayel's aides and bodyguards, was killed immediately and, in spite of the return fire, the four assassins were able to make their escape.

Then came the third, conclusive episode in this unfolding drama. A bus carrying a number of Palestinians, with their wives and children, set out from the meeting place in Corniche Mazraa to return to the refugee camp at Tal Zaatar. Perhaps he was late, perhaps he lost his way, but for whatever the reason, the driver strayed from the normal route through all-Moslem suburbs and took a short-cut through Ain Rumaneh. There, the vehicle was spotted by Phalangists, who decided to use it to take their revenge for the death of their comrade. The Phalangists opened fire on the bus from two sides, and in the first volley more than a dozen people were killed. By the time the shooting ended, twenty-seven people had died and nineteen were wounded. Those who were injured and the very few people who were unhurt were trapped in the bus for two hours as the attackers shot at any movement and prevented anyone going to the aid of those inside. Only after the intervention of more senior Phalangists were ambulances and Lebanese security men allowed to go to the scene.

It was, quite clearly, a cold-blooded massacre out of all proportion to the incidents which had sparked off the affair. Coming so soon after the events in southern Lebanon and the uncompromising statements of the Right-wing leaders, it seemed to many to be part of a deliberate Phalangist policy to force a confrontation with the Palestinians. If that were so, it succeeded very well, for the massacre was immediately denounced by the Palestinians in the strongest terms. A statement made the dangerous charge that 'this was a pre-planned act, prepared with the knowledge of the Phalangist Party leadership, and timed to coincide with the presence of the President of the Republic in hospital' – President Franjieh had gone into the American University Hospital in Beirut for a gall bladder operation a few days earlier.

Yasser Arafat, regarded as the most moderate and temperate of all the Palestinian leaders, sent a cable to Arab heads of state calling the affair 'a bloody massacre by the armed gangs of the Phalangist Party ... a flagrant conspiracy with imperialism and Zionism'. The Arab Liberation Front, the Iraqi-backed and very extreme commando group which lost eighteen of its members in the attack, talked about 'the treacherous Phalangist hirelings implementing what Israel wants'. Ominously, they promised vengeance. The presence of the large number of members of the A.L.F. may have had something to do with the Phalangist action, for the Corniche Mazraa meeting was being run by yet another small splinter organization, the Popular Front for the Liberation of Palestine – General Command of Captain Ahmed Jabril, the people actually responsible for the Kiriat Shmoneh attack in which eighteen people died. The P.F.L.P.–G.C. and the A.L.F. were at this time members of what became known as the Rejection Front – the alliance of Palestinian dissidents who took the most uncompromising stand and opposed any idea of a negotiated peace with Israel. These groups were the most disliked and feared of all by the Phalangists because of their extremism, and if indeed the Ain Rumaneh massacre was planned even a few hours in advance then the fact that it was the Rejection Front which was to be the target may well have weighed with those who laid the ambush.

Now it was the turn of the Phalangist leadership to be on the defensive. Gemayel himself offered to accept the arbitration of representatives of other Arab states who were invited 'to uncover the whole truth about this painful incident, to establish what is right, to end the bloodshed, and to draw up a formula of reconciliation and co-ordination between Lebanese and the Palestine Resistance'. And in a second statement Gemayel offered a face-saving formula, suggesting that it was some outside agency, 'a third force', which was responsible for deliberately fomenting trouble between Lebanese and Palestinians. Yet for all his attitude of sweet reason in public, the Phalangist leader was taking a much stronger line with his own followers. In his paper, *Al Amal*, Gemayel wrote:

We have reached a situation in Lebanon in which the State is overcome. The State has renounced its responsibilities and sovereignty, and this has given rise to unofficial mini-States and armies which are undisciplined and whose identities are not known. Worse, there are certain areas in Lebanese territory and in the hearts of towns which are outside the framework of every authority, even the authority of the resistance movement.

We do not accept that there should be any authority above the authority of the Lebanese State. We do not accept that there should be areas outside the authority of the Lebanese State. I emphasize that, had the law been applied justly and rightly to all, we would not have reached the current situation, which is due to the application of the law to one group and failure to apply it to others.

For all its apparently moderate tone, Gemayel's comments were in fact directly inflammatory, as it was the presence of the heavily-armed commandoes in the refugee camps and the inability of the Lebanese State to exert its authority there that lay at the root of the Rightists' case. The Phalangists had always distinguished 'good' commandoes from 'bad'. They considered, or said they considered, Yasser Arafat and his organization, el Fatah, as the only proper channel for commando activity. And they abhorred both the more extremist groups of the Rejection Front and the other main body, the Syrian-backed Saiqa, which they saw as a foreign fifth column in their country.

Whatever the reaction of the leaders, the men with the guns on both sides had no doubt of the seriousness of the situation or about what they should do. Within hours of news of the Ain Rumaneh massacre spreading around the city, road blocks were going up in every quarter, and exchanges of mortar and heavy machine-gun fire began in what were to become 'the traditional fronts'. Ain Rumaneh and the neighbouring Moslem suburb of Chiah were at the centre of the battle, while fighting was raging too around Tal Zaatar and in Christian Dekwaneh, with skirmishing breaking out wherever there was what the military call 'an interface', an area where supporters of the rival parties lived side by side or came into close proximity. Nor was the fighting confined to Beirut. On the day after the killings in Ain Rumaneh, Tripoli suffered as much as the Lebanese capital, and in Sidon, Tyre and dozens of other towns there were clashes between Right and Left, Christian and Moslem. So swiftly did the situation deteriorate that the normally lethargic Arab League became alarmed and dispatched the Secretary-General, the former Egyptian Foreign Minister,

Mahmoud Riad, to Beirut to offer his services as a mediator. Mr Riad did meet with some success, for after only one meeting he was able to persuade the Phalangists to hand over two of the men said to be responsible for the massacre of the bus passengers. They were named as Maroun Chitti and Hanna Amin Oun and, with thirteen others arrested by the security forces, they were kept in police custody. The Palestinians welcomed the move, which certainly did a lot to defuse the situation, but on the ground passions were running high and the battles went on. It was not until the following Wednesday evening, three days after the original trouble, that the Government and Mr Riad were able to get all the leaders and the local commanders to agree to a ceasefire, the first in the long series which was to mark the progress of the war.

As both sides drew back, the cost of this first brief round was assessed: at least ninety killed, three hundred wounded, and more than £20 million of damage caused by the mortar bombardments, the fires and the looting which had gone on for three days. On both sides, there was a realization that the battle, if it was to be followed through to the end, would not be like the comparatively minor engagements of the past. The Phalangists were better organized and stronger than they had even been, and the Palestinians could muster thousands of men and clearly had plenty of arms and ammunition – their steady mortar barrage on the Christian suburb of Achrafiyah, a place of no military significance, showed that.

For the Phalangists, it was the beginning of what they saw as the battle of their homeland, the battle for continued Christian survival in the Arab world. They wanted, if they could, to maintain their privileged place in the Lebanese hierarchy, but even more basically they wanted to preserve Lebanon as a special case in the Middle East, an enclave of moderation and Western-oriented thoughts and ways in an area looking increasingly to the East. They believed Lebanon had a particular role to play and knew that, if the Palestinians were allowed to dominate the country, that status would rapidly disappear.

The Palestinians, for their part, had no real desire to fight in Lebanon. Their leaders realized that the diplomatic gains of the past could all be lost if they became embroiled in

Lebanese domestic politics or bogged down in a costly war. The Lebanon was not their home, nor did they want it as a new homeland. They were committed to the idea of returning to Palestine, of establishing a state there. To do that, they had to have a base and they knew very well that Lebanon was the last place left open to them. They had been brutally expelled from Jordan five years earlier, and the memories of that savage experience were still vivid. They had to preserve their one safe haven and they had to show that they could not be dominated or suppressed by anyone, least of all by the weak Lebanese State or the unofficial Phalangist Party. The Palestinians had to fight, but for their leaders it was a sad decision which they sought to avoid. Only among the young tearaways on both sides was there any enthusiasm for the battle, and the months of constant combat were to bring about a change even in them. For the moment it was with reluctance that the Palestinians prepared for the conflict, while the Phalangists looked forward with some eagerness to reasserting the authority of the Lebanese in their own country.

3

The Palestinians – catalysts of conflict

When the Palestinians first began arriving in Lebanon, neither they nor their hosts could have had any inkling of the trouble this trickle of refugees was to bring. For it was no more than a trickle at first, usually made up of the people least likely to cause trouble – those with special skills, members of the professions or businessmen who could easily integrate into the Lebanese social structure. The Palestinian exodus from their homeland began in 1948, in the wake of the first Arab–Israeli war, and was caused as much by the actual fighting as by Israeli efforts to dislodge the indigenous people. Most of those who moved at this time – from Haifa, Jaffa, and the surrounding villages – went only as far as the West Bank, forming their own refugee communities around Ramullah or Jericho, or to Gaza. It was only later, after the 1956 and 1967 wars, that the great mass movement of the Palestinians began and, as the camps of Jordan filled, the overflow went on to Lebanon, to be reinforced three years later by hard-core Palestinian activists when King Hussein subjugated the commandoes in his country.

The first refugee camps in Lebanon were set up around Beirut, an indication of how little notice the authorities of the time were paying to this small influx, for in the 1970s it was to become clear that the ring of camps around the city could strangle the capital and enable the Palestinians to cut the main road communications with the rest of the country. In 1948 and in the following years, as the refugees kept arriving, the Lebanese policy was to give a qualified welcome to those able and willing to integrate, though always regarding them as second-class citizens, while sweeping the very poor, the dispossessed and those with no particular skills to offer into the camps, where they were out of sight of the majority of the

43

people and certainly far from the homes of members of the political and business establishments. Out of sight and out of mind, for in the camps things were happening that were quite unknown to the Government. In Lebanon, just as in Jordan, the fledgling Palestinian commando organizations went to the camps to find their recruits and supporters as well as ready-made secure bases from which to operate. As early as the beginning of the 1960s the camps were becoming the centres of radical Palestinian thought, the embryo arsenals of the armed movement which was soon to be launched, and the breeding grounds of the dissatisfaction and determination to return to their homeland which the emerging leaders so carefully fostered.

The commando movement was actually born in the Gaza Strip, that jam-packed tongue of Egyptian territory extending into Israel which contains nothing but orange trees and refugees – 350,000 of them. Yasser Arafat, who was born there in 1929, was one of a number of young men who met to discuss what could and should be done, and, unlike many similar groups, this one actually did something, for when the plotters split up and went off to Egypt, the Gulf and the other Arab states, Arafat and his colleagues kept in touch, and by persuasion, cajolery and argument, managed to interest men who had money, or had access to weapons or to those who could supply them. Thus was born al Fatah, the main guerrilla group; its name is a reverse acronym of its Arabic title: Harakat al-Tahrir al-Watani al-Filistini, the Palestine National Liberation Movement. Before this, a more formal organization had been officially voted into being by the first Palestine National Congress, which met in Jerusalem in 1964 and set up the Palestine Liberation Organisation, headed by the lawyer and demagogue Ahmed Shukairy and run by a fourteen-member Executive Council. At the same congress, a Palestine National Fund was founded, which was to finance the P.L.O. and its agencies, and a few months later an Arab summit conference in Alexandria established the Palestine Liberation Army, which became known as the 'regular forces' of the Palestine Resistance Movement, though in practice the Army was always under the control of the country in which its units were stationed.

44

Right from the beginning it was al Fatah which made all the running. It launched its first offensive action on 1 January 1965 with an attack into Israeli-occupied territory from Jordan. This had not been the original plan; it had been intended to send the first mission into Israel proper and Lebanon was naturally chosen as the jumping-off ground, but as early as this, when Fatah was only a few months old, the Lebanese authorities were already eyeing it with suspicion and one of the commandoes who was to have made this first thrust was arrested by the Army. A month later there was a bland announcement that the man concerned had committed suicide while in prison, an unlikely event which was immediately denied by al Fatah, which said the commando had been tortured to death. There were protests and demonstrations in the camps, but there was nothing the Palestinians could do, for at this stage they were still few in number, with only a handful of the more simple weapons, meagre ammunition, rudimentary organization, and little but the goodwill of their compatriots and the hostility of their enemies to sustain them. Still, they kept up the attacks, and in mid-1966 came the first reported armed clash between the guerrillas and the Army in southern Lebanon, an engagement which not surprisingly the Army easily won. Soon afterwards came an incident illustrating the tiny numbers engaged in commando activity at this time, for Yasser Arafat himself was among a group of *fedayeen* (literally: men of sacrifice) arrested as they were about to cross into Israel from Lebanon. It was only through Syrian pressure that Arafat was released after spending some time in the Sands Prison in Beirut, but the remarkable thing was that the commander-in-chief of the Palestinian forces should think it necessary to take part personally in a hazardous mission. There may have been an element of bravado about it, for the Palestinians, like most Arabs, are highly impressed by the 'macho' image and proof of personal bravery has to be given by any leader. Arafat had already taken part in missions into occupied territory from Jordan and was constantly having to demonstrate his personal disregard for danger, as he moved not in the classic revolutionary style of a fish in the stream but rather as a grain of sand in the Arab machine, an irritant which no-one liked and many tried to expel. Thus Arafat's personal participation in the attempted raid could have been due to the lack of numbers of trained men available, and perhaps also to a desire on the leader's part to see if his style of militant diplomacy could persuade the Lebanese Army on guard along the border to turn a blind eye to what was going on, for the pragmatic Arafat was well aware that his men's arrogance and unwillingness to consider any point of view but their own, even at this early stage in their revolutionary history, were often responsible for the troubles which came their way.

A year later, in May 1967, came two more incidents which seriously exacerbated relations between the Palestinians and their unwilling Lebanese hosts. Two separate groups of commandoes returning to Lebanon after raids into Israel were arrested, and one man named Ata Daabara later died in prison. The various Lebanese authorities put out conflicting explanations of how the man had met his death, while Fatah again charged that he was the victim of torture by the Deuxième Bureau. There were protest marches from the Ain Helweh camp near Sidon, the first public demonstration by the Palestinians in Lebanon, and even some support from various Lebanese individuals and parties, so that the Government was forced to appoint a commission of inquiry. Though this body eventually and predictably exonerated the authorities, the affair left a nasty taste and was perhaps the first step in the long series of incidents which led to the full-scale war between the two sides.

The Six Day War in 1967 marked the beginning of public Arab acceptance of the commando movement, for after the massive, swift and humiliating defeat of their regular Armies, the Arabs needed some body on which to pin their hopes. Suddenly the commando movement became fashionable; what the massed regular forces could not accomplish, the guerrillas would, and the image of the *fedayeen*, the carefully nurtured picture of a young man with a *keffiyah* around his head and face, a rifle in his hand and a burning determination to liberate his homeland in his soul, was a romantic concept which appealed to the youth of every Middle Eastern country. So the numbers of fighters gradually increased, with the vast majority of them stationed in Jordan, a country still officially at war with Israel and one which appeared determined to regain its own lost territory. Lebanon, on the other hand, had given up no land in the war and was plainly not going to do any fighting at any time if it could possibly avoid it.

Yet the build-up of the Palestine Resistance Movement was still a slow process, and the commandoes were better at swaggering around Amman than at infiltrating enemy lines or causing losses to the Israelis. Then came an unlooked for opportunity which did far more for the Resistance Movement than any raid it could have staged. Overnight, the *fedayeen* were transformed into everyone's heroes and the reason, in the usual paradoxical Arab way, was that the guerrilla forces had taken part in a set-piece battle with the Israelis in which they had, quite naturally, been beaten. This legend-making affair was the Battle of Karameh, a small, pleasant town of white stone and small gardens on the bank of the River Jordan near the Allenby Bridge. A group of guerrillas had established their base there, and the Israelis decided to move in and clean out this nest of 'terrorists'. A strong raiding force was assembled, and on 21 March 1968 one group crossed the river by the pontoon bridge which had replaced the original Allenby Bridge, another crossed by the Damia Bridge to the north, while a third unit was landed by helicopter behind the town. Confident of their success, for they rarely met any real opposition from the still divided and ill-prepared Arabs, the Israelis had made little effort to conceal their preparations, and for days past their newspapers had warned that vengeance would be exacted for the latest commando attack, in which a school bus was blown up in the Negev and two children killed. So confident were the Israelis that they had even laid on buses to take selected journalists into the town while they conducted their search-and-destroy operation there. This time, things went wrong. The Jordanian Army had made its own dispositions, with artillery zeroed in on all the approaches to the town, while tanks had been moved into position in the surrounding hills. So, when the Israeli armour rolled forward with its tail of soft-skinned troop-carrying vehicles, the Jordanian gunners were able to take a considerable toll of the attackers. In the town itself, the Israelis did not have it all their own way either. The Israeli troops who landed from the helicopters were caught in a hail of cross-fire from the machine-gun positions set up by the Palestinians and, though the better trained, more disciplined and efficient Israeli soldiers were able to prevail, they suffered heavy losses.

Immediately the fifteen-hour Battle of Karameh was over, the Palestinian propagandists swung into action: they proclaimed it as a great Arab victory at a time when the Arabs badly needed some encouragement. There was little mention of the crucial part played by the Jordanian Army; rather it was the desperate image of Palestinian commandoes firing their red-hot machine-guns until the ammunition ran out and then throwing their grenades before dying at their posts which was carefully put out by the Palestinians. Total Israeli casualties were admitted to be twenty-eight dead and seventy wounded, though many thought they must have been higher than this, while the Palestinians said they had lost more than one-hundred-and-seventy men on their side – probably an exaggeration. Yet morally, the battle was certainly won by the Palestinians and their potent myth-making machine quickly took full advantage of it. Soon recruits were pouring in to join Fatah, and in Jordan and in Lebanon the still basically hostile governments had to adopt a far more careful attitude to the way they dealt with their awkward guests. In Lebanon the Palestinian population had now reached 250,000, with some 90,000 people in the fifteen camps scattered around the country, each with its commando affiliations and commando presence, so that the number of operations launched from Lebanese territory was mounting steadily. In the Arkoub, the barren, rocky wasteland around the foot of Mount Hermon, on the border of Syria, Israel and Lebanon, the Palestinians were setting up permanent bases, using the hundreds of caves there to store ammunition and the few villages as their supply centres, much to the annoyance and fear of the local people. Not a week went by without some guerrilla activity, raids to blow up water culverts used by the hard-pressed Israeli farmers in the *nahals*, the armed settlements in Upper Galilee, ambushes of border patrols, grenades thrown at buses and lorries, roads mined and rockets fired across the border.

At the same time, the leaders of the movement were establishing offices in Beirut and Amman, organizing training camps and supply bases, and sending envoys around the world to drum up support wherever it could be found. They were trying, too, to sort out their own differences and to forge a new image of their movement which would be acceptable to the world beyond the Middle East as well as to the Arab states. The first step was to get rid of Ahmed Shukairy, a ranting figure who had done little to unify the movement or make it effective, though he had done a great deal of international harm by his wild oratory: he is best remembered for his promise to 'throw the Jews into the sea' at a time when the Palestinians hardly had the strength to catch the few bones of support thrown to them. So, at a meeting of the Palestine National Council in Cairo some three months after the Karameh turning point, Shukairy was quietly and efficiently voted out of office and Arafat was elected. As Arafat had already become leader of al Assifa (the Storm), the military wing of el Fatah, he was now in a virtually unassailable position. He had control of the money and of the regular forces of the movement through his chairmanship of the P.L.O., and of the guerrilla forces through his command of Fatah. It was a position he quickly consolidated, for Arafat was always much more a politician and diplomat – only his admirers would say statesman – than a revolutionary leader in the style of Castro, much less of Guevara. His early participation in raids into enemy territory, though occasionally necessary, must have been dictated by the need to establish a reputation. Once that was done, he was free to concentrate on building up his own position and that of the forces he represented: the moderate, middle of the road section of the Palestinian Movement. Arafat reinforced his authority by putting his brother, Dr Fathi Arafat, in charge of the Palestine Red Crescent, the 'Army Medical Corps' of the Movement, which was also responsible for assessing injuries and paying indemnities to those wounded or to the dependants of men killed. He also saw to it that a special fund set up by Kuwait to pay compensation and pensions was under his direct control, and in a third significant move he took over the command of the Palestine Armed Struggle Command, P.A.S.C., the military police of the Movement. He turned this force into his own private army, better paid, better trained and better equipped than the usual run of guerrillas, with recruits carefully chosen to owe loyalty directly to Arafat. This unit was to prove useful in quelling mutinies and arresting dissidents when necessary and was always the most disciplined and reliable of the Palestinian forces.

However, in spite of the new surge of support for the Palestinians, they still faced difficulties in their two main theatres of operations, Jordan and Lebanon. In Jordan, the King was gradually moving towards direct opposition to the commandoes and the bloody confrontation which was forced on him by Palestinian intransigence and the need to preserve his realm. In Lebanon, the much weaker and more hesitant Government was more concerned about Israeli reprisals than with the arrogance and lawlessness of the commandoes themselves, though it, too, was forced to act and in March 1968 it passed a law forbidding 'infiltration by Lebanese or Arab nationals living in Lebanon into territory occupied by Israel'. This step by the Lebanese Government was clearly designed more to mollify the Israelis than to have any practical effect. The Lebanese wanted to say: 'Look, it's not our fault. We've told these people they are not allowed to attack you. Now please leave us alone.' For, of course, the tiny Lebanese Army, some 14,000 strong, was quite incapable of securing the border with Israel and was well aware that, in the new conditions created by the Battle of Karameh, any forceful action against the guerrillas would lead to demonstrations of support, perhaps riots and direct involvement on the side of the Palestinians, by about half of the Lebanese population. Nevertheless, the Army did intervene when it came across some blatant instance of the law being flouted, and there were a number of occasions on which clashes developed between Army units and commandoes on their way to or from Israel. Just as regularly, Israel sent patrols into southern Lebanon to blow up houses suspected of being used by 'terrorists' or shelled guerrilla camps, often doing more damage to farms than to the widely dispersed *fedayeen*.

Then, in December 1968, came the first of the massive Israeli 'reprisal raids' against Lebanon, which were clearly intended as much to force the Lebanese to act on Israel's behalf against the commandoes as to 'punish' the country for the unwilling shelter it was giving to the Palestinian fighters. The excuse for this first show of Israeli strength was an attack by two men of the extreme Popular Front for the Liberation of Palestine on an El Al airliner in Athens in which an Israeli engineer was killed. Picking an appropriate target, the politicians in Tel Aviv sent a helicopter-borne task force to Beirut Airport, where thirteen aircraft and a petrol storage tank were blown up, and damage totalling an estimated £500 million was caused. The raiders met with no opposition at all; at one point, an Israeli officer pulled a cowering airport gendarme from under a desk and demanded some Lebanese 25-piastre pieces so that he and his men could get some soft drinks out of a machine, a remarkable display of propriety amidst so much devastation.

The Israeli attack on the airport was universally condemned and, if its sole purpose had been to cause damage, it was not much of a success, for the Lebanese collected huge amounts of insurance and Middle East Airways was quickly able to re-equip itself to become one of the most modern and profitable airlines in the area. On another level the raid achieved all that was planned, for there was an immediate outcry in Lebanon against the complete lack of action by the Army and the utter failure to protect the airport or to move against the raiders during the time they were there. The Moslem and Left-wing parties, and of course the Palestinians, charged the Army with negligence at best, collusion at worst, and kept up a barrage of criticism. The Right and the Christians argued that the Army did not have time to take effective counter-measures and anyway could not keep a sufficient force in every part of the country where Israel might find targets. As the heated debate went on, the lines were drawn for the long-running clash of views which was to lead to so much trouble. The radical parties argued that the role of the Army was to defend the country and everyone in it, while the Right said that, given Lebanon's capabilities, the only defence was to remove the causes of the Israeli attacks, a task the Army should be given. The Left answered this by pointing to the long-standing fear in Lebanon that Israel wanted to annex the south of the country up to the Litani river in order to secure adequate water supplies for Upper Galilee – a dream long abandoned by the Israelis, if it was ever seriously entertained.

The students, who had their own grievances and were in

general in sympathy with the aims of the radical parties, began a series of strikes, ostensibly to protest against the Army's lack of effective action, in reality to push forward the reforms they wanted, which amounted to no less than a change in the whole Lebanese system. All that they did manage to achieve at first was to bring down the Government of Abdullah Yafi, which was soon replaced by a new administration formed by Rashid Karami, the strongest of all the Sunni Moslem leaders. Yet the students' strikes and demonstrations did focus attention on the issues before the country, though for the majority of the people the question at this time was the simple one of whether or not the Palestinians should be allowed to conduct their operations from Lebanese territory.

As the debate went on and the smouldering antagonisms came increasingly into the open, Mr Karami, a realistic man who could see the logic of both arguments, was forced to resign. He acknowledged that there were two sides in Lebanon, the first time any politician had accepted the polarization of the country, and he counselled a 'neutral' stand by any government to avoid causing a split among the people. He must have seen the impossibility of this, for to be 'neutral' a government would have to abdicate all responsibility and take no action to curb lawlessness or to check the conflicts between the two sides which were bound to develop – though in fact this was very nearly the attitude adopted by some later governments, notably the disastrous régime of Rashid Solh immediately before the outbreak of the civil war. As it was, the dispute became more bitter and began to take on what were called 'confessional overtones', that is the supporters of one side were almost all Moslems and began adding the basic demands of their community to their arguments in favour of freedom of action for the commandoes, while on the other side the Christians not only wanted the commandoes to be curbed but they also wanted stronger action against the radical Lebanese parties which they saw as a threat to the established order, and in particular to the dominant position of the Maronites.

So the debate went on, with the President and the Prime Minister adding to it when they differed publicly over what should be done. The President, Charles Helou, a weak leader who relied entirely on the Army for his support, had been elected largely because he was pledged to carry on the policies of Fuad Chehab, his tough predecessor; he was not expected to take any initiative of his own, but on this occasion, perhaps at the prompting of the Deuxième Bureau which formed the secret government of the State, the President made a radio speech coming down strongly and unmistakably on the side of those who wanted no more commando action from Lebanese soil. Mr Karami, a Moslem, could not allow himself to be identified with a régime which seemed to be openly espousing only the Christian point of view and so he had to go. He later agreed to resume the Premiership if the President abandoned those parts of his speech dealing with the commando problem, and came up with his own solution of the matter – 'co-ordination' between the Army and the commandoes – though how this was supposed to mollify the Israelis or avoid future punitive raids he did not explain.

While the politicians wrangled, the situation on the ground deteriorated. There were curfews in Beirut and other major cities, and constant clashes between the Army and the commandoes. One of the worst clashes came in April 1969, when the Army surrounded a commando base in the southern village of Kfarkalla, killing a number of Palestinians. There was an immediate protest march in Sidon, which was banned by the Government, went ahead anyway and led to forcible attempts by the Security Forces to suppress the demonstration. Eleven people were killed and dozens hurt as the trouble spread throughout the country; the Army began moving more openly against the Palestinians, and in Beirut the Phalangists went into action beside the Army. On one occasion Phalangist militiamen and Palestinian guerrillas traded fire across the Place des Martyrs, the main square of the commercial area of Beirut, as housewives were crowding the *souks* and shops. In Tripoli, the Army precipitated a crisis by demanding that commandoes remove an unauthorized building they had erected in the Nahr-el-Bared refugee camp. The commandoes refused, and the Army began shelling the densely populated area. As the fighting went on, with a new outbreak coming in a different part of the country as soon as one was contained elsewhere, no politician seemed capable of solving the crisis and a series of mediators had no greater success.

Then in October came a major outbreak with Tripoli closed down, Beirut the scene of urban skirmishes, and every other town and city declaring for one side or the other, largely according to the religious persuasion of its inhabitants. In Tripoli, however, came the beginning of a new dimension in the quarrel, for the fighting there was not only between the Army and the Palestinians, it was also between the supporters of Mr Karami, whose fief this was, and the followers of Farouk Mokaddem, a Sorbonne-trained lawyer who had ambitions to wrest political control of this important base from Mr Karami in order to launch his own radical movement. To add to the confusion, Syria closed its border with Lebanon in support of its traditional policy of causing as much trouble to its neighbour as possible – every Damascus régime still harboured the dream of a Greater Syria, which would take in Lebanon, a dream which was to play its part in the formulation of Syrian policy when the Lebanese civil war broke out. There was also Syrian jealousy of Lebanon, which by greater efficiency and more forceful commercial practices was siphoning off trade which had traditionally gone to the Syrian ports of Latakia or Tartous. An immediate reaction to all this came from Iraq, which offered any support needed to the Palestinians in Lebanon – a Pavlovian reaction caused more by Syria's moves than by the plight of the commandoes, and one which in fact had no practical effect whatsoever.

As the fighting spread to the whole country, it was clear that the Army could not suppress the commandoes and at the same time maintain order in the towns and cities; equally, it was obvious that the Palestinians did not have the strength to win an all-out confrontation, even if they wished to embark on such a wild adventure. Some compromise had to be found and after the intervention of President Nasser's chief trouble-shooter, Hassan Sabry al Kholy, both Yasser Arafat and General Emil Boustany, Commander of the Lebanese Army, agreed to meet in Cairo to hammer out some sort of accommodation. The fruits of their conference came on 3 November 1969 after two days of talks. In a joint communiqué they announced that agreement had been reached and a way found to end the battles. There was an immediate ceasefire, and both sides retired to lick their wounds and to prepare for the further clashes which both knew were bound to come. Perhaps, if the Cairo Agreement had been observed to the letter by the Army and the Palestinians, the interval before a new outbreak of fighting might have been longer, though it was clear that continued Palestinian presence in Lebanon would be bound to bring Israeli retaliation, and those Israeli raids would in turn lead to Right-wing attempts to remove the cause of the attacks or to ensure that the Palestinians were so reduced that they were unable to mount any 'dangerous' actions. One small difficulty, besides the major ones of the directly opposing policies of the two sides, was that the Cairo Agreement itself was never published, so that all concerned could put what interpretation they liked on it and claim, whenever it suited them, that the other side was breaking the fragile pact. In fact, the Agreement was a remarkable victory for the Palestinians and a complete climb-down by President Helou and his Army backers, who in effect had to accept Karami's idea of 'co-ordination' and also had to promise the commandoes much greater facilities. It was formally laid down that the Palestinians could have control over the fifteen refugee camps in Lebanon, could use them as bases, and could install weapons there. The movement of commandoes to and from the border was to be facilitated, and the supply route to the Arkoub (a track leading from Syria through Deir al Achayer and Rachaya known as the Arafat Trail) was to be kept open. This was a considerable gain, for a major Army objective had been to cut this route, and there had been fierce fighting as the Palestinians seized border villages and even put in frontal attacks on the Army post in the old crusader fort at Rachaya as they sought to keep their lifeline to the south intact. On the Army side, the advantages were few: the Palestinian leaders promised to exert their authority over the lawless elements in their ranks, though both they and the Army knew they were powerless to do so without provoking a war within a war; they undertook to see that commandoes did not go armed or in uniform in Lebanese towns; and they agreed to give up a small and unimportant base at Dniyyah in North Lebanon. Perhaps the only useful clause from the Lebanese point of view was a paragraph laying down that 'the Lebanese civil and military authorities will continue to exercise their full rights and responsibilities in all Lebanese regions in all circumstances'. It did not mirror the facts of the situation at the time or at any stage in the future, but it did at least provide a legal cover when the Army felt strong enough to move against the commandoes again.

So ended the first major trial of strength between the Lebanese Right and the Palestinians. At the end of the day, as an accounting was made, it was not this time the physical damage or even the cost in life and limb which was reckoned up. What was important seemed to many to be the respective strengths of the two sides, for no-one doubted that this was merely a preliminary bout and that the full struggle was yet to come. On both sides there were unpleasant lessons to be assimilated, though on balance it was the Right which found itself worse off. The Palestinians had shown tenacity in the various engagements, they had deployed large numbers of sophisticated modern weapons and had shown that they knew how to use them, and that they had plenty of material. More important, events had demonstrated that, if any conflict went on for more than a day or two, the Left-wing parties and the traditional Moslem groups would join in. The split in the country of which Karami had warned had become a reality of political life and would have to be taken into account whenever in the future Right-wing leaders tried to pursue nationalist and élitist aims.

There were a few lessons for the Left too. One of them was that the cherished notion that Moslem troops in the Army would never act against them was not true. That myth was exploded at a village called Yanta. Hours after a new ceasefire had been announced, a group of commandoes on a hill above the hamlet began mortaring a company of the Lebanese Army encamped below. Immediately, the Moslem Captain in charge sent two platoons to deal with the mortars. The soldiers, both Moslem and Christian, carried out the operation in textbook style, killing nine commandoes and taking the rest prisoner. And when asked why he had launched the operation after a ceasefire, the Captain replied: 'My orders were not to take offensive action, but to defend myself. When my men are being mortared, my idea of defence is to remove the sources of the fire. That is what we did.'

The Palestinians also realized that the whole might of the

Army had not been deployed against them and that the Christians had yet to muster all the men at their disposal. Nor were they entirely convinced that in another context the Lebanese Government might not seek outside aid. After all, President Chamoun had called in the American Marines in 1958. Could the same thing happen again? So, in the stock-taking by both sides, there came the realization that the troubles which had plagued the country for most of the year had been no more than a rehearsal for what was to come, and a probing of each side's capabilities and intentions. The battle lines were being drawn, though there was still a hesitation; concessions and accommodations by the protagonists might still have prevented the conflagration. But neither was in a mood to compromise and the opportunity was lost; from 1969 onwards, it was downhill all the way.

4

Taking sides

One of the factors leading to the bitter enmity which developed
between the Resistance Movement and the Lebanese Right
was that not all the commandoes were members of Fatah or
shared the moderate views of Arafat. There was a powerful
group of fringe organizations which frightened the Lebanese
Christians and the old-guard conservative Moslem leaders
alike. These were the avowedly Marxist bodies which all
stemmed from the Arab Nationalist Movement created by Dr
George Habash in 1953. Habash, a dedicated revolutionary,
was driven out of his home in Lydda by the Israelis in 1948
and with his family had to walk to Jerusalem. From there he
went to Beirut to study medicine, and it was in the freedom
of Lebanon that he and a number of other intellectuals formu-
lated their ideas of revenge on the Israelis, liberation of all
people from oppressive régimes and economic backwardness,
and the unity of the Arabs. With Habash from the beginning
were the two men still carrying his message to every part of
the Arab world: Ahmed Khatib, who has been a constant
thorn in the flesh of the feudal rulers of Kuwait, and Wadi
Haddad, who has become the most extreme of them all, a man
whose responsibility for so many hijackings, assassinations
and terrorist attacks has made him Israel's most wanted
enemy.

Habash himself went off to Jordan as soon as he qualified
to set up a free clinic for the people of the refugee camps. The
squalor and misery he saw there, coupled with the indifference
of the Jordanian authorities, led directly to the establishment
of his Popular Front for the Liberation of Palestine (P.F.L.P.).
This was born in 1967, when three smaller groups combined,
though the A.N.M. (Arab Nationalist Movement) had men

operating inside Israel for a long time before that and had the forethought to plant a large number of 'sleepers' (agents who would live normally and peacefully until they were needed for some special operation, perhaps years after first being put in place). Habash and his men believed firmly in the concept of the world revolution and preached that 'the road to Tel Aviv runs through Amman, Riyadh, or Beirut'. They were as keen to sweep away the 'reactionary' Arab governments as they were to free their homeland; they were prepared for a long guerrilla war and took as their model the Vietnamese, while Habash himself regarded North Korea as the ideal modern revolutionary state. Such ideas were anathema not only to the Right-wing Christian establishment in Lebanon but also to the traditional Moslem leaders, who were as opposed to any form of 'Godless Communism' as their Christian opposite numbers. Early on, Habash was put in prison by the Syrians and spent seven months there, until his followers mounted an ostentatious rescue operation; in Lebanon, the party was banned, yet managed to form an alliance with Kamal Jumblatt's Progressive Socialist Party; in Jordan, the P.F.L.P. was the main target when King Hussein's Bedouin Army moved against the guerrillas, for it was Habash's men who organized the mass airplane hijackings which led to the confrontation.

Habash is a man of immense charm and personality, a man who might have become the undisputed leader of all the Palestinians but for his religion and his extremism: he is a Christian, a member of the Greek Orthodox Church, and no Christian can hope to command the support of all the Palestinians, the majority of whom are Moslem. Habash would also have had to change his views to become a popular leader, for dedicated Marxism is still not understood in the Arab world and the masses of the people have little love for any form of Communism. Another factor militating against any popular appeal by Habash is his unwillingness to compromise any of his political ideals; he believes in the purity of his concept, and will not allow any deviation from the line and policy laid down. This led in 1968 to the first split in the Popular Front: Ahmed Jabril, a former Captain in the Syrian Army who had fought with el Fatah and then transferred to Habash's organization, left to form his own group, the oddly named Popular Front for the

Liberation of Palestine – General Command. In the following year came the second defection when Nayef Hawatmeh – a dedicated Palestinian fighter, a Marxist extremist who is a Christian from Salt, a town on the East Bank of the River Jordan – broke away to form the Popular Democratic Front, which he himself described as 'the Left wing of the Popular Front, as opposed to the *petit bourgeois* group led by Habash'. These two erstwhile friends, who still shared the same revolutionary aims though they differed on how to achieve them, now proceeded to fight it out in the streets of Amman, and it was only the intervention of the despised forces of Fatah which put an end to this 'war within the revolution'.

It was in Jordan that the commandoes had to fight for their lives as King Hussein reluctantly and under pressure from the hard-liners in his Army and his own family moved against the Palestinians, breaking their power in the 'Black September' of 1970 and finally crushing them the following year. The King's move had a profound effect in Lebanon, for this small country of a mere three million people now became the sole refuge of the militant Palestinians. Beirut was the only city in which they could establish their offices and move freely in public; the Lebanese border was the only one open to them for operations against Israel; the Lebanese countryside was the home of their training centres and supply bases; and the refugee camps provided the cover and protection needed for their operations' headquarters, the arsenals and the homes of their leaders. By no volition of its own, Lebanon became the last haven of the Palestine Resistance Movement and had to pay a high price for it. Certainly there was some respite as the Palestinians fought desperately to hold their position in Jordan, and, seizing the opportunity of their heavy commitment there, the Lebanese felt able to impose some new conditions on the commandoes – they were prohibited from firing across the Lebanese border into Israeli territory, they were not allowed to lay mines anywhere along the frontier, and they were banned from carrying arms in built-up areas. Of course, incidents still continued and there was an increasing tendency for the Phalangists to become involved even in the most minor affairs. It was a remarkable sight to drive through crowded Beirut streets after word of some new Palestinian 'outrage' had spread and to see the respectable, blue-suited businessmen of the quarter standing outside their shops or offices with automatic weapons held casually at their sides. For the enmity of the Phalangists towards the Palestinians was not diminished by the savage defeat these displaced people had suffered in Jordan. Rather, there was rejoicing that one Arab government at least had the will and the ability to curb the trouble-makers; for, though nothing was ever said in public, in their private meetings and whenever the Phalangists held their get-togethers the leaders lost no opportunity to prepare their followers for an eventual show-down in Lebanon. Israel, too, played its part, keeping up a steady series of cross-border raids, bombing refugee camps and often killing Lebanese as well as Palestinian civilians, for the poor Lebanese who were forced out of their homes in the South by the Israeli attacks frequently found shelter on the fringe of the camps around Beirut, or in Nabatiyeh or Sidon in the South. So the Phalangists and, to an increasing extent, their allies of Camille Chamoun's National Liberal Party had plenty of ammunition for their diatribes against the commandoes; and they felt more able to speak of the conflict they were sure was approaching because of a Lebanese domestic development. In September 1970, the six-year term of office of President Helou came to an end and a new President was elected – elected in a very Lebanese way, for the counting of the votes produced a remarkable scene. Under the Lebanese system, the President is chosen by a simple majority of the ninety-nine Deputies of the single-chamber Parliament, so that fifty members could elect the new Head of State; and that was just what happened when Suleiman Franjieh and Elias Sarkis ran for office. But, as the clerk read out the voting figures, the Speaker, Sabri Hamadeh, tried to rule that fifty out of ninety-nine was not in fact a majority. Franjieh went for his gun, while one of his supporters tried to hit the Speaker, whose own bodyguard drew his pistol. For a moment all was confusion and there was the very real possibility of a gun-fight between the Parliamentary Deputies to be watched live on television throughout the country. At the last moment Hamadeh conceded that fifty was in fact a majority and declared Franjieh elected. It was a close thing and showed the depth of feeling in the various camps. The point at issue was that the members of the 'Nahj', the supporters of the former President Fuad Chehab, wanted to ensure that one of their own people was elected and that Chehabist policies would continue, just as they had done during the reign of Charles Helou. Sarkis was the Chehabist, Franjieh the new broom determined to break the power of the Army and in particular of the Deuxième Bureau, which still ran the country.

Franjieh was a very different man to his predecessor, the soft, worldly Charles Helou, who was more at home speaking in French than in Arabic, a journalist and poet, a man at his best in the *salon* atmosphere of the rich aristocracy. Franjieh was a Godfather figure, a tough man from the North Lebanese mountain town of Zghorta, where his family was the predominant one among the five ruling clans. Originally, Hamid Franjieh, the eldest son, was supposed to have carried the family's political standard and Suleiman was to have remained the feudal leader in their northern home. However, Hamid was struck by a heart attack and never recovered, so Suleiman had to go into politics in his place – not hampered at all by a two-year forced exile in Syria after he had gunned down members of a rival family while they were at their prayers one Sunday.

Franjieh's main strength as he had canvassed for support was his promise to restore law and order in the country, with the clear implication that he would also apply the law to the commandoes, who were blamed, often unfairly, for most of the banditry which was becoming a feature of everyday life. As one cynical Deputy was to remark about Franjieh years later: 'He was elected to use his muscle, and instead he tried to use his brain.' There was an early opportunity for Franjieh to show what he could do, for only a week after he had assumed office came the death of Gamal Abdel Nasser, the one towering figure on the Arab scene. Immediately the Egyptian leader's supporters and admirers in Lebanon decreed a forced three-day period of total mourning. Within an hour of the announcement of the great man's death, men with guns visited every hotel, restaurant, bar, café and shop in the main towns of the country and ordered their closure. At the same time, a barrage of gunfire began, the traditional Arab way of either celebrating or mourning. This steady stream of bullets into the air continued for three days, by which time twenty-six people had been killed by stray shots and hundreds wounded. It threatened to continue and there were signs that the Nasserites might be preparing to exploit the situation, perhaps even considering a coup against the fledgling régime. Franjieh recognized the challenge and met it head-on. He ordered the gendarmerie, the 'mountain police', into Beirut, Sidon, Tyre and Tripoli, the main centres of disturbance. Demonstrations and marches were banned, and the police efficiently enforced the order. The trouble-makers got the message, and the incipient revolt was over before it had begun. Franjieh had come through his first test with flying colours and stored up for himself a reservoir of goodwill among all sections of the people – a store of respect he was to dissipate with profligate abandon over the six years of his incumbency.

It was the Franjieh régime as much as the presence of the commandoes which brought about the confrontation everyone had expected for so long. In the Lebanese system it was recognized that high office was the way to found a family fortune and no-one thought any the worse of people who took advantage of that; but there were limits. In the case of the President, it was accepted that he would accumulate wealth in the last two years in office, though not in all six. Nor was it expected that the nepotism everyone knew would follow a change of régime would become quite so blatant. For a start, the President's parliamentary seat at Zghorta was taken by his son Tony Franjieh – again, not an unusual occurrence. Then young Franjieh was made Minister of Posts, a promotion so rapid that even Lebanese eye-brows were raised; and in that capacity, Tony Franjieh proceeded to turn the Post Office and all its ancillary services into a monument to total inefficiency. The Lebanese postal system had never been noted for speed of delivery and the telephone network was a wonder understood by few, but under the new Franjieh régime complete collapse was obviously close. This gave the Minister the opportunity to plead that lack of equipment was the source of all the trouble, so that he could enter into large new contracts with foreign suppliers. The problem was that few of the contracts were ever signed, as international concerns baulked at the 'commission' the Minister demanded – in many cases he sought twenty-five per cent of the equity of the companies which were to get the orders.

Nor was Presidential patronage limited to his own family; anyone from his home town of Zghorta who had supported him in his bid to make his family pre-eminent there was sure of a job – the Mayor, Ramez Khazen, became the Director of the Ministry of Information, which he rapidly changed into a publicity office for his patron and thus destroyed any credibility or value it might once have had. Even the most hardened criminals could count on being helped: two men sentenced for particularly nasty robberies in which murders had been committed were freed by Presidential decree and were later frequently seen in the Presidential entourage. At the same time, the Franjieh clan were securing interests in all the most profitable Lebanese firms. After a bomb had been set off at the works of a mineral water factory, the directors of the concern issued a statement saying that, contrary to public rumour, the President's son was not on their Board, a denial of doubtful accuracy aimed at preventing any further attacks.

Yet the President did begin his régime by trying to curb the lawlessness plaguing the country. To show that he meant business, a convicted murderer was hanged, the first time a death sentence had been carried out in Lebanon for many years. And to display the impartiality of the régime, soon a second man had to be executed. Even in death, the confessional balance in the country had to be maintained. For it was on this balance of the religious communities in Lebanon that the precarious edifice of power was based, enabling successive régimes to exist. The system was laid down soon after the country's independence from French rule in 1943, but harked back to older times, when the country was a province of the Ottoman Empire. Under the Ottoman method of administration, the various religious communities in the provinces were given a considerable degree of autonomy, guiding their own affairs, subject only to the overriding authority of a governor. Jews and Christians were not only tolerated in Ottoman times but actively protected, though Moslems still had preference when it came to such things as public appointments, apportionment of land and so on. In the mid-nineteenth century the structure

began to break down in the provinces around the eastern
Mediterranean, and there were a number of cases of inter-
communal rioting which brought the condemnation of the
European powers on the increasingly hard-pressed Ottoman
Empire. To allay the criticism, the administrative machinery
was overhauled, and in Lebanon the sub-provinces or *vilayets*
of Tripoli in the North and Sidon in the South were combined
with Beirut, and it was decreed that the Governor should be
a Christian subject of the Empire, who was to rule with the
help of a council on which Christians would hold a majority
of seven to five over Moslems. It was clearly this ancient pre-
cedent which the Lebanese negotiators had in mind when they
met soon after independence to draw up 'the national covenant', a document with no legal force or binding power, but
one which enabled the different communities to get along with
each other, to a greater or lesser degree, for some thirty years.

At the time this blueprint for the future of the country was
drawn up, it was believed that the Maronite Christians in
Lebanon formed the largest single group (they are followers
of St Maron, and form an autocephalous church in com-
munion with Rome). For this reason it was laid down that the
Maronites should always furnish the President of the Republic
and, as all the Christians combined were thought to exceed
the total number of Moslems in the country, it was also provided that Christians should outnumber Moslems in the ratio
of six to five in all the institutions of the State: in Parliament,
the Civil Service, the Judiciary and the Armed Forces. To
further the system of balances, if not checks, the Sunnis, the
largest Moslem sect, were to provide the Prime Minister; the
Shia had the Speakership of the House; and the Deputy
Premier and Deputy Speakers were to be from the Greek
Orthodox group. In the Army, just as in civilian life, posts were
filled according to an officer's religion, so that the Army commander was always a Maronite and the Chief of Staff a Druze.
In the Army, however, the proper proportion was always more
difficult to maintain; there was no conscription, so often there
was a majority of Moslems joining up, as in every country it
is the poorest and those who cannot find work who usually
turn to the Army for employment. Yet, because the commander was always a Maronite, this preponderance of

Moslems in the ranks was not reflected in the officer corps; at the outbreak of the civil war, sixty-two per cent of the officers were Christians and their power was even greater than the figures would indicate, for almost all the senior positions were held by Maronites, and the thirty-eight per cent of Moslem officers were largely confined to the junior ranks.

Over the years, the demographic pattern in Lebanon changed: the birth rate was slightly higher among the Moslems, particularly in the Shia community, while on the Christian side the numbers emigrating were much greater than from the Moslem communities. It is estimated that there are as many Lebanese outside the country as in it: three million people scattered around the world, though most of them are in North and South America where they form powerful pressure blocs; the first American Senator of Lebanese origin was elected a few years ago. As the make-up of the population changed, so demands came for a new formula to apportion power. The Shia, through the Imam Moussa Sad'r, sought a much bigger share, maintaining that they were now the single largest group in the country; what they overlooked was that, because of their deprived status in the past, they just did not have the men of education and talent necessary. The Sunnis, still led by the conservative establishment which had helped to draft the National Covenant, had no desire at all to see any amendments made, fearing that such moves would whittle away the power of the traditional leaders and provide opportunities for the younger and more radical elements. On the Christian side, there was an even greater determination to resist change; for the Christians, and the Maronites in particular, any alteration to the Covenant would mean a diminution of their influence. So eager were succeeding Maronite Presidents to hold on to what had been given to the Maronite community that even such an elementary step as the holding of a census was blocked, and some thousands of once-nomadic Moslem Arabs who had settled years before in the Wadi Khaled area in the north-east of Lebanon were consistently denied citizenship as their numbers would have provided an instant and readily seen addition to the Moslem half of the country.

If a group of peaceful Arab farmers like the people of Wadi

Khaled could cause dismay, the arrival of some 300,000 Palestinians in Lebanon, the huge majority of them Moslems, spread something like panic, and not among the Christians only, for the old Sunni leaders realized that their position could easily be threatened by such numbers. The early reaction on both sides was to keep the Palestinians away from Lebanese affairs, to make sure they were physically segregated in their camps if possible, and to deny them the full rights and privileges enjoyed by citizens of the country. The various crises over the years, the armed confrontations and the political in-fighting, were primarily to achieve these ends, though in the process other forces came into play, and the skilful propaganda of the Palestinians carefully used the divisions in Lebanese society to bring about a polarization and to draw the Lebanese Left into an alliance with the commandoes. It was not difficult to do this, for the blatantly inequitable distribution of wealth in the country, the display of luxury next to examples of the direst poverty, and the way in which the rich were getting richer and the poor poorer provided a classic theatre of operations for those wishing to exploit the situation. Lebanon must have been one of the few countries in the world where patients taken to hospital could opt for first-, second- or third-class operations – and had to produce the money before a surgeon would reach for a scalpel. The minimum monthly wage in the country in the early 1970s was L.L.240.00, then equivalent to about £30; at the same time rents were going up fast as the newly rich of the Gulf poured in to spend their sudden wealth in a profligate display of ignorance. Nor was it only the comparatively well-off who were affected by this boom, for thousands of Syrian labourers were brought in to work on the building sites of apartment blocks and luxury hotels, and their high wages made it difficult for the lower paid Lebanese to compete for decent accommodation. While all this was going on, successive governments resorted to higher taxes on cigarettes, increased fees for the thousands of bureaucratic functions in which every citizen was involved at some time, and introduced more efficient on-the-spot traffic fines as a means of raising revenue, largely because methods of direct taxation were in total disarray – it was a rare millionaire in Lebanon who paid more than a tiny fraction of what he owed.

67

So the material was there, ready to be exploited; and the next major clash between the Army and the commandoes brought about a new situation. It came in 1973, only months before the Arab–Israeli war was to bring change to all the Arab states, so that international events soon reinforced the pressures for reform in the Lebanon. Not that the years between 1969 and 1973 had been ones of total peace: in 1970, for instance, great efforts had to be made to calm things down after the aggressively Christian villagers of Kahhaleh, on the main Beirut–Damascus highway, had ambushed a convoy of commandoes escorting the body of one of their fallen comrades back to Syria. Using a church, among other places, as a vantage point, the villagers poured fire into the open jeeps of the Palestinians as they negotiated a bend in the road; seventeen *fedayeen* were killed and many more injured. On that occasion, the situation was probably saved because the Minister of the Interior of the day was Kamal Jumblatt, leader of the Progressive Socialist Party, who enjoyed better relations with the Palestinians than any other Lebanese politician, largely because he was more in sympathy with them than was anyone else, and because they rightly saw in him their main ally if it did come to a show-down. Jumblatt was another of the many Lebanese anachronisms: a feudal landowner from an ancient aristocratic family, he was a hereditary leader of the Druze people as well as the country's leading Left-wing politician. He was also a millionaire and a mystic who made regular trips to India to sit at the feet of his own private guru, an intellectual with a considerable knowledge of the literature of various cultures, an ascetic among men dedicated to the pleasures of their rich life, and a wily politician ever on the look-out for personal and party advantage. Jumblatt was too difficult and prickly a man to last long in any Lebanese government, but such was his power that no administration could survive without his consent and over the years he established himself as the rallying point of the Left, a role which complemented his feudal power in the Druze territory of the Chouf in south-eastern Lebanon, and added to his friendly relations with the Palestinians, so that he emerged as one of the three or four most powerful men in the country.

In 1971 and 1972 it was Israeli raids in southern Lebanon

and bombing attacks on Palestinian camps which again raised the tension between the Lebanese and the commandoes, though the incidents were contained with what amounted to only minor loss of life and damage by Lebanese standards – for all its veneer of civilization and sophistication, Lebanon was basically a series of primitive feudal societies where life was cheap and tribal warfare an everyday experience. The political leaders and their supporters were brought up on the idea of violence and saw it as a natural part of existence; the Israeli raids, the regular clashes between the Lebanese and the Palestinians, the casual shootings and bombings which took their toll each day, all these were accepted and caused none of the outrage which would have followed if anything similar had occurred in any Western country. So these years were accounted fairly peaceful, for all the lists of casualties in the papers – forty-eight killed in an Israeli raid on Hasbaya, forty when the Israelis strafed Deir al Achayer, others killed or maimed as a spate of letter bombs was sent to people, over one hundred slaughtered during a massive Israeli sweep of the south of the country in retaliation for the massacre of the Israeli athletes at the Munich Olympics. The list grew daily, but only when some incident led to widespread fighting and threatened to lead to the civil war which was approaching so inexorably did either the Lebanese or other Arab governments become alarmed.

Such a moment came in April 1973, when a thirty-strong unit of the special Israeli 'counter-terror' force slipped ashore at Dead Man's Beach on the southern edge of Beirut to join six of their undercover comrades waiting with a fleet of hired cars. This assassination squad went to an apartment block on Rue Verdun, just opposite one of the Internal Security Forces' barracks. The attackers shot the two young commando guards on duty at the entrance to the building, then stormed upstairs; they found three targets: Youssef Najjar, the Fatah leader responsible for liaison with the Lebanese authorities; Kamal Adwan, in charge of Palestinian operations in the Israeli-occupied territories; and Kamal Nasser, the official spokesman of the P.L.O. who was much better known as the poet of Ba'athism, the new revolutionary-nationalist ideology of Syria and Iraq. The three men were gunned down; so too was Youssef

Najjar's wife as she tried to protect her husband, an elderly Italian lady who opened the door of her apartment to see what was going on, and two Lebanese security men who bravely but foolishly went to see what all the shooting was about. The Israelis – commanded by a blonde young woman, according to several people who watched from neighbouring apartments – failed in their main objective, which was to kill Salah Khalaf, Arafat's deputy, who was known as Abou Iyyad and who was the first leader of the notorious Black September organization, the small band of dedicated Palestinian extremists who believed they could achieve their aims by indiscriminate terror attacks. Khalaf and Arafat had been in the apartment an hour earlier, as they held a strategy meeting with the other three, but had left in response to an urgent and mysterious summons to Damascus.

If the Israeli raid did not succeed as completely as its planners had hoped, it exceeded their hopes in another way, for it led to the worst confrontation between the Lebanese and the Palestinians before the civil war itself. The new fighting, which came hard on the heels of the Israeli attack and as a direct consequence of it, was also due to a growing split between the Sunni Moslem establishment, led by the Prime Minister of the day, the powerful Saeb Salam, and President Franjieh and the Maronite leadership. Salam claimed that he had repeatedly telephoned the Army Commander, General Iskander Ghanem, while the raid was in progress, to demand that troops be sent to intervene; nothing had been done. Salam described this as insubordination and inefficiency, and demanded Ghanem's dismissal. President Franjieh refused, so Salam himself resigned and claimed in a series of speeches that the Franjieh régime was turning the country into a Maronite fief, and that the Moslem Prime Minister had no share in running the country. The Sunni community supported Salam, but the President would not budge, and over the months underlined his contempt for the opinions of the Moslem political and religious leaders by nominating four Prime Ministers who did not have the whole-hearted support and approval of their own people – first the dithering Amin Hafez, then Takieddin Solh, Rashid Solh and Nureddin Rifai.

The immediate consequence of the Israeli raid was a rise

in tension between the Army and the commandoes, with both sides making quiet preparations for a show-down which soon became a headlong rush to battle: guerrillas were arrested for carrying arms near the American Embassy, always one of the most closely guarded places in the country; and, in an apparently deliberate policy move, security forces picked up members of the Popular Democratic Front wherever they could be found. Arafat and the other Fatah commanders were anxious to avoid any new fighting, but Nayef Hawatmeh of the P.D.F.L.P. had no such inhibitions; his men kidnapped three soldiers to serve as hostages for the release of the commandoes, then found that the Army was in no mood to negotiate. Instead, General Ghanem set a deadline for the release of the soldiers – and probably did not even wait for the time he had himself set before ordering his troops to attack Palestinian positions in the camps and in various areas around Beirut, in the South, and at a camp just north of the capital. This time it was the Army which was eager to settle matters once and for all, as even the release of the three captured soldiers, arranged by Kamal Jumblatt, and a reported ceasefire pact between the Palestinians and the Government, did nothing to stop the fighting. In most cases it was the Army which was doing all the attacking, while the commandoes were merely trying to hold on to previously established positions; among the Palestinians and the Lebanese Left there was a general conviction that the Government was trying to do what King Hussein had done in Jordan three years earlier, to suppress the Resistance Movement once and for all. In a broadcast President Franjieh denied his government was trying to stage 'a black May', while warning that he would not tolerate 'an army of occupation' on Lebanese soil, a fairly pointed indication that he intended to follow the matter through to the end. That was certainly how the commandoes saw it, for the next day fighting intensified all over the country, with the guerrillas now taking the initiative by attacking Army positions in the Bekaa Valley in the East and in the South. The guerrillas felt able to go over to the offensive because they had been reinforced by units of the Palestine Liberation Army stationed in Syria, who had been sent by President Assad to help their hard-pressed colleagues. In the face of this threat and the obvious hostility of the régime in Damascus, the Lebanese Army took the calculated risk of escalating the conflict by bringing in the Air Force. Hawker Hunters and Mirage jets were used to strafe commando positions in the Bekaa and in the north of the country, where the Palestinians were shelling the Klaiyat military air base; then, to demonstrate the use of air power where the largest possible number of commandoes could see its effects, the planes were used against camps on the outskirts of Beirut itself and at the Sports Stadium near the airport, where the Palestinians seemed to be gathering for an attack on the International Airport, already closed by commando rockets. The concentrated salvoes from the planes, the equivalent of a broadside from a destroyer, were too much for the Palestinians. Under the guise of accepting the mediation of Arab diplomats who had hurried to Lebanon to offer their services, Arafat sued for peace.

In this round of what was in effect the continuing war between the Lebanese and the Palestinians, the Lebanese had come out on top and had slightly improved their position, for the commandoes had to make a number of concessions and to agree to a much stricter observance of the Cairo Agreement than there had been in the past. What was much more important, however, was the way in which the 1973 clashes brought about the polarization of the country and led directly to the full-scale civil war of 1975. Palestinians and Moslem radicals alike were convinced that the central policy of the Army, and thus of any régime which had a Maronite President, was to break the Resistance Movement in Lebanon. The Christians, particularly the Phalangists, Camille Chamoun's followers in the National Liberal Party, and the supporters of the Franjiehs in the North believed that it was only outside intervention which had prevented the Army from finishing the affair on this occasion; and they began making their preparations for the final round they were sure would come.

There was a split, too, between the erstwhile allies of the establishment. In the past a Maronite President had always been able to count on the support and co-operation of the Sunni Moslems, who provided the Prime Minister and thus had a vested interest in the continuation of the traditional order. Now, however, the conservative Sunni leaders felt themselves slighted; Saeb Salam said openly that President Franjieh's aim was to reduce the power and influence of the premiership, and thus to whittle away the position of the whole Moslem community; and in apparent confirmation of this, Franjieh chose yet another weak candidate for the office once the ineffectual Amin Hafez finally resigned. This time it was Takieddin Solh, a member of a family which had played an active part in the struggle for Lebanese independence, but a man with no personal following or power base and by no means one of the recognized leaders. He was forced to form a Cabinet in which every possible shade of opinion was represented and every political bloc had its nominee; with such a cumbersome administration it was not surprising that nothing at all was achieved, and the gradual slide to anarchy began, as all sides set about making their own preparations for the ultimate confrontation and took very little notice of the Government.

At first there were few signs of the process of disintegration which was so surely beginning; on the contrary, the Arab–Israeli war in October 1973 led to a period of frantic expansion and boom for Lebanon as a result of the sudden huge rise in oil revenues which followed the Gulf States' decision to use their resources to back the combatants. Many of the oil producers were small sheikhdoms which in the past had existed on fishing or producing millions of multi-coloured postage stamps; they had neither the knowledge nor the capacity to absorb the millions of dollars suddenly pouring into their coffers, though their rulers had quite enough sense to know that the old ways of handling money were long past. So they turned to the bankers of Lebanon, men who spoke their language, understood the courtesies and conventions needed to transact financial affairs, and were capable of advising them and acting as middlemen in their careful investments. The Lebanese were not the only ones to realize the possibilities; so, too, did the financiers of many other countries, but, because of the Lebanese banking laws, they could not move in and set up on their own behalf. The only way to get a foothold, a share of the huge amounts of cash flowing through Beirut, was to buy into local banks and this is what happened. In 1973 and 1974 there was a procession of Swiss, German, French, British and Arab financiers knocking on the doors of the established banks. At the end, only twenty-five of the eighty banks in Lebanon remained under wholly Lebanese ownership; sixteen were controlled by other Arab interests and thirty-six by foreign institutions (three of the licences issued were in suspense).

Not only bankers were trying to get into Lebanon – so was everyone else who saw a possibility of creaming off some of the oil money; brokerage houses, investment counsellors, trade representatives and all the rest poured in, and even the number of money changers with their booths in every main street showed a sharp increase, for the suddenly wealthy people of the oil-producing states invaded Beirut in unprecedented numbers, not only to spend the summer away from their hot and dusty homes as they had in the past but also to attend to their affairs, to buy apartment blocks or to set up businesses. With them they brought their families, servants and retainers, so that the oil money was being spread around at all levels, and even the smallest fish in the financial sea could get their share of what was going. It was only those outside the circle who suffered and in Lebanon in these years that meant the poorest section of the population, those whose wages remained fixed while prices shot up astronomically, for the Lebanese system of *laissez faire* capitalism led to galloping inflation, and the policy of non-interference pursued by the Central Bank meant a growth in the money supply without any regulatory action by the Bank to mop it up. These were the boom years for many, but they were years of increasing hardship and disaffection too, which added to the pressures building up, and the division of the country not only into Christian and Moslem, Left and Right, but also into rich and poor; and though it may have been coincidence that it was the Moslem section of the population which had the greatest share of the have-nots, this was a fact which had its effect.

5

The war begins

The fishermen's dispute in Sidon and the Ain Rumaneh massacre a month later were merely the curtain-raisers to the civil war, and were soon to become comparatively minor incidents, though at the time they assumed huge significance, so that the men of goodwill on both sides and the Arab mediators so free with advice all did their best to prevent these two events bringing about a full-scale conflict. Yet it soon became clear that others had quite different aims: on both Left and Right there were groups who had decided that the time was ripe for the final battle, and they were not going to allow the politicians to take the opportunity away from them. On the Christian side, the Phalangist leaders at this early stage were being as moderate and reasonable as they thought possible. Pierre Gemayel knew he had gone as far as he could by handing over two of the men responsible for the Ain Rumaneh shooting and had to insist that if they were to be tried then there should also be a full investigation of the incidents which led up to the ambush, as well as that attack itself. If the Phalangist leader had gone any further, he would have lost his standing in his party, and the respect and high esteem in which he was held; and the Phalangist party without the moderating hand of Gemayel would have been a desperately dangerous machine. Now it was Kamal Jumblatt and his Progressive Socialist Party who were making all the running, while the Palestinians were doing what they could to stay on the sidelines. Jumblatt had become the leader of what was known as the 'National Front', a coalition of some fifty Leftist parties in Lebanon, of which his own was merely the largest; and this new political alliance now issued a direct challenge to the Right by laying down that Front representatives in Parliament would refuse to vote for any government in which Phalangist Ministers were included. In the Lebanese system, the Prime Minister is nominated by the President after informal consultations with the Deputies, and the man chosen then forms his Cabinet. That done, the Prime Minister and his team have to present themselves to Parliament for the approval of the Deputies, and if a Prime Minister fails to secure a vote of confidence then he either has to resign and allow someone else to take over or to make another effort to form a Cabinet acceptable to the Deputies. Because of this system, any combination of the major parties could frustrate efforts to form a government. The result was that the various Cabinets always contained representatives of those parties, and took as the planks of their policy platform the causes which the different groups espoused.

In seeking to 'punish' the Phalangists for the Ain Rumaneh massacre by excluding them from any government, Jumblatt was obviously provoking a trial of strength and at first the Phalangists seemed eager to accept the challenge. Gemayel ordered his two Ministers in the Rashid Solh Cabinet to resign, and with them went their three allies from Camille Chamoun's National Liberal Party and Majid Arslan, a Druze bitterly opposed to Jumblatt. The defection of six Ministers meant that Rashid Solh had to go, though he tried desperately to cling to power until forced out on 15 May, when he immediately gave a practical demonstration of what he believed the consequences would be. His own stronghold in Beirut was an area bordering Zarif, and it was there that he went after making his farewell speech to Parliament. He drove up in a car escorted by a large van and, as his supporters gathered around him, he personally opened the doors of the van – and began handing out a consignment of modern rifles to his grateful admirers.

With Jumblatt insisting that the Phalangists should not participate in any new government, and the Phalangists for their part making it plain that without them there could be no Cabinet, there was political deadlock. But on the ground things were moving fast and, in comparison to the early moderation of their leaders, the Phalangists were showing themselves as intransigent and as brutal as their opponents. For it was the Right-wing which saw to it that the tension was

raised whenever a lull in the constantly erupting clashes persuaded people it was safe to go out on the streets once more
and to try to resume some sort of normal life. Time after time
the hesitant return to work was halted when one or two shots
from a carefully concealed sniper killed some innocent passer-
by. Immediately, the militiamen of both sides rushed to their
positions and began exchanging fire, each thinking the other
responsible for the incident, while the hard-pressed Security
Forces did their best to root out these *agents provocateur*. The
majority of the snipers were Phalangist supporters and there
was direct evidence that their actions were a deliberate plan
by the military leaders of the Phalange to keep the trouble
going: one of the snipers was named François, and he was no
Lebanese, but an imported French mercenary, an unsavoury
specimen who was hired for the express purpose of sowing dis-
sension. His qualifications were that he was a superb shot and
that he had no qualms at all about killing men, women or
children, if that was wanted by those who paid him. He was
himself killed a few months later and there were few to mourn
him. Another man who later admitted he had been responsible
for killing or wounding some forty people was a Christian
doctor whose surgery overlooked a bridge regularly used by
people going from predominantly Moslem West Beirut into
the mainly Christian Eastern sector of the city. He said he
killed out of blind hatred of Palestinians and Leftists, and
made the remarkable claim that he could distinguish such
people from the mass of ordinary Lebanese. This man sur-
vived, and was not regarded as anything more than slightly
eccentric by his friends and colleagues. Another significant
detail which pointed to a deliberate Rightist policy of provocation was that, whenever the Security Forces did manage to
capture or kill a sniper, the man was never identified. Given
the basically Christian Maronite composition of the Army
command, this was taken as a tacit admission that it was
the Phalangists who were spreading terror and ensuring the
continuation of the fighting.

Not that the Left and the Palestinians were blameless. On
the contrary, they were guilty of worse excesses; the difference
was that the Palestinians and the Left were robbing, looting,
murdering and burning out of sheer lawlessness, with brigands

and outlaws crowding into Beirut, Tripoli and Sidon to take advantage of the situation for personal gain, rather than acting out of any ideological convictions. That made it no better for the victims: the approaches to Beirut had become regular ambushes which people either had to try to crash through at speed, with the consequent danger of death in a hail of gunfire, or to negotiate their way past, handing out huge sums to be allowed in or out of the city. The latter method was just as dangerous, for the sight of money often awakened new greed and the man offering a bribe was summarily killed so that all he had could be taken, rather than the mere portion he offered. There were terrible incidents of brutality, as well: Christians thought to have connections with any of the Right-wing parties were tortured and mutilated before being killed; women were raped in front of their husbands; children saw their parents beaten, and did not themselves escape death because of that. Such incidents led to reprisals, and the reprisals led to worse excesses. It was the beginning of a shameful tradition of the most utter and depraved brutality, a callous disregard for human life and a willingness to use the foulest methods of torture and murder which was to go on throughout the war, and to be adopted by all sides.

As these lone incidents of killing and terror went on, the war-fronts of Beirut erupted once again. There were mortar and artillery duels between the Palestinian camps of Tal Zaatar and Jisr al Pasha, and the nearby Christian suburbs; on the northern outskirts of the city the Phalangists began their long battle with the poor Shia, Kurds and Syrian day-labourers who lived in the slum districts of Karantina and Maslakh, 'protected' by units of some of the most extreme Palestinian groups. The Shia of Nabaa were drawn into the conflict and, as the fighting spread, soon it was only the Armenian community of the city, concentrated largely in the suburb of Bourj Hammoud in an area surrounded by Phalangist-dominated districts, which managed to stay aloof.

With no government and no prospect of any government, the situation seemed hopeless, as both sides adopted more and more uncompromising policies. On the Right, there was also the emotive interference of the Maronite Church. The newly elected Patriarch, Antonius Khreish, had tried to keep out of

politics, realizing the harm which had been done by his predecessor, Cardinal Paul Meouchi, who had never hesitated to
speak up for the Maronites on any controversial issue. Now
the new Patriarch let it be known that the exclusion of the
Phalangists from government was 'unacceptable' to the
Church. And to reinforce the involvement of religion, Father
Charbel Kassis, head of the Maronite Monastic Orders and
unofficial head of the Phalangist 'think tank' which drew up
their often extreme manifestos, for once came into the open
and made a series of tough statements supporting the Phalangist position. The Maronite monks, he said, were willing
to put all their resources at the disposal of those willing to
defend Lebanon and Lebanese sovereignty. And to show that
this was no empty boast, pictures appeared in all the newspapers of the Brothers, their *soutanes* tucked up above their
knees, running to take up positions around their monasteries,
Kalashnikov rifles in their hands.

While fighting went on all round Beirut and spread to many
other parts of the country, Kamal Jumblatt maintained his
firm opposition to any Cabinet which would include Phalangist representatives and so made the formation of a government of traditional balance impossible. His intransigent attitude showed for the first time the deep differences between the
Druze leader and his allies, the Palestinians, and those he
should have been courting, the Sunni Moslem politicians. Both
these groups were quite ready to see the ban on the Phalangists
lifted, even though it was the Palestinians who had suffered
directly from the Rightist attacks, and it was in revenge for
Ain Rumaneh that Jumblatt had first applied his veto. The
commandoes and the Moslem leaders realized that, by preventing the formation of a new administration, Jumblatt was
merely leaving the way clear for President Franjieh to produce
his own solution; and that is just what he did. On 23 May
came the announcement of the new Cabinet chosen by the
President: it was headed by Nureddin Rifai, a retired general
whose last post had been Commander of the Internal Security
Forces; the new Minister of Defence was the current Army
Commander, General Iskander Ghanem, a man highly suspect
in the eyes of the Left; and, with only one exception, all the
other Ministers were serving Army officers. The President's

move was strictly constitutional, for he had the legal power to choose what Prime Minister he liked, and the Prime Minister could pick his Ministers. All that was required was that they should go before Parliament to obtain a vote of confidence from the Deputies. Yet the President had ignored the conventional steps normally taken before a new Cabinet was selected; there had been no consultations with Deputies or leaders of the various parties and blocs, and no attempt to seek the usual political balance. All that had been done was to preserve the confessional aspect, as the various officers chosen included representatives of the Maronites, Greek Orthodox, Greek Catholic, Druze, Sunni and Shia Moslems. This extraparliamentary Cabinet may have seemed to the President and his advisers a neat way out of the apparent constitutional *impasse* he was facing, and in countries with a different history and background might have been acceptable. In Lebanon, there had never been a military government and the Army was identified, rightly or wrongly, entirely with one faction in the continuing war. There was no hope of the 'Cabinet of Generals' being accepted – a fact made clear within hours of its installation as celebratory gunfire echoed around the Christian areas of Beirut, while in the Moslem districts new barricades were built, burning tyres blocked off the streets, and militiamen hurried to take up their positions for the concentrated Army-Rightest attack they expected to follow.

Clearly the President had underestimated the strength of opposition to any military take-over of the country, in whatever form it was presented, for the immediate effect of this Cabinet was just the opposite of what was wanted by the Right-wing, which of course included President Franjieh. Kamal Jumblatt, who had found himself drifting further and further away from his Palestinian allies and Sunni Moslem friends, immediately repaired his fences with these bodies and, within twenty-four hours of the new Cabinet's formation, Jumblatt had joined with such traditional leaders as Rashid Karami, Saeb Salam and Raymond Edde in firm opposition to the President's move. Sheikh Hassan Khaled, the Mufti of the Republic and spiritual head of the Sunni community, sank his differences with the Imam Moussa Sad'r to call for the resignation of Nureddin Rifai, while in Damascus the Syrian Government made plain its opposition to what seemed to be an Army take-over; the Palestinians, still claiming not to be interfering in internal Lebanese politics, made no official comment, though their attitude was obvious; for once, the whole of the Left and all the Moslem groups were in agreement.

General Rifai and his Ministers resigned three days after taking over, and in their brief period in office naturally achieved nothing; what did stem from the President's attempt to impose his own government on the country was the further polarization of Left and Right, Moslem and Christian. The Phalangists, the National Liberal Party and the Maronite Church were all as one, which was to be expected; the important factor was the bringing together of the Leftist alliance of Kamal Jumblatt with the basically traditional and conservative groups led by Salam and Karami. The division of the country was becoming clear and complete.

With the departure of the Rifai Cabinet, the way was open for one of the traditional Premiers to be called upon and, having been so soundly defeated, the President had no choice but to call on the strongest of them all, Rashid Karami. Anticipating the move, Karami had made his plans: when his appointment was announced, not a single shot was fired in celebration, a remarkable and unusual display of discipline, a sign of the new Prime Minister's power, and a signal that he intended to be leader of the whole country, rather than the representative of any faction or religious persuasion. Yet the mere designation of a new head of government could not halt the anarchy and two days after Karami's appointment a burst of gunfire in crowded Riad Solh Square in the heart of the commercial district marked the beginning of new urban battles, though they had been going on in the suburbs the whole time. Now the fighting spread to the south of Beirut, following the killing of Naim Burdkan, Commander of the National Liberal Party's militia, with the Christians of Damour battling it out with the Moslems of neighbouring Naame. In Beirut itself lawlessness prevailed and few roads were safe – the Saudi Arabian Ambassador's car was hit by bullets as he was on his way to see the President, and diplomats and politicians alike had to share the hazards experienced by everyone living in the country.

As Mr Karami set about his Herculean task of forming a

Cabinet acceptable to all parties, the fighters on both sides continued to skirmish. A wave of kidnappings of Christians in Moslem areas spread panic in Beirut and led to reprisals and the taking of hostages on the other side – in Kahhaleh, on the Damascus Road, the Christian villagers stopped every car coming through and arrested any Moslems they found. At the end of the day, more than one hundred hostages were being held prisoner under the wavering guns of two very scared fourteen-year-old guards. On the battle-fronts things were quieter, though both sides held their positions; but the calm was short-lived, and was broken in a very Lebanese way. Two young Iraqis, probably members of one of the commando groups, tried to pick up a pretty young Christian girl in Ain Rumaneh. Her many brothers went out looking for the two to avenge the insult to their family honour, firing their guns in the air as they did so, of course. That was enough; soon the whole district was in flames again, and the warning shots from rifles had changed to mortar and rocket bombardments between Chiah and Ain Rumaneh. The noise of the battle prompted the nervous militiamen on both sides in nearby areas to start their own fights, and soon the whole of Beirut was in turmoil once more, with nowhere exempt from the violence. Mortar bombs fell near an office being used by Arafat and prompted a return barrage on the Phalangist headquarters in Sioufi, where Pierre Gemayel was directing operations. With the fighting now concentrating on the port and the commercial district the already serious damage there turned into mass destruction, with both sides pouring in tremendous fire-power to wreck buildings and installations and damage beyond repair what had taken years to build.

The Iman Moussa Sad'r, regarded by many as one of the few honest and sincere men in the country, began a fast to death in a mosque in the centre of the city, vowing to stay there until the violence ended. His gesture lost a little credibility a few days later, however, when an explosion at a Palestinian training camp in the Bekaa Valley killed more than forty people, all of them found to be young Shia followers of the Imam. He was forced then to reveal the existence of a new Shia militia called Amal (Hope), which he said was to be used to defend southern Lebanon against Israeli attacks, though it seemed to many to be just one more fighting force on the already crowded scene. A way out for the Imam was found when Rashid Karami announced that he had been able to form a new Government. It was made up of only six members, and was to last for more than a year, though only on rare occasions in that period was it in any way effective. Camille Chamoun was brought in as Interior Minister to represent the Phalangists as well as his own party; Karami himself took the Ministry of Defence and, in a move designed to reassure the Left, arranged for General Ghanem's early retirement. For once things looked better. And then came an incident comparable to the row over the flirtation between the Christian girl and the Iraqis in Ain Rumaneh: in Zahle, the main Christian town of the Bekaa Valley region in eastern Lebanon, two men were playing with a pin-ball machine in a café: one was a Moslem, one a Christian. An argument began and, in the manner accepted as normal in this anarchic land, one of the men took a grenade from his belt and threw it. Others joined in, and eight people were killed before the affair was brought under control. The police for once acted quickly and arrested three of those involved. The three were, however, Christians in a Christian town and soon a huge crowd besieged the police station, demanding their release; the police gave in, and new battles began as the Moslems of the villages surrounding Zahle expressed their own points of view. The battles spread to Beirut and to Tripoli, and now it was the turn of this northern city to be closed and shuttered and given over to the gunmen. There had been violence in Tripoli before – a wave of bomb explosions had destroyed most of the shops owned by Maronites, and even those of the long-established Greek Orthodox merchants had not escaped. The result was that most Christians had left Tripoli, which had always been a predominantly Moslem town. Now it came under attack from neighbouring Zghorta, where the President's son, Tony Franjieh, had formed his own ultra-Right militia, the Zghorta Liberation Army. So the odd spectacle was presented of the President and the Prime Minister in Beirut meeting regularly and apparently trying hard to bring an end to the war in the country, while in Tripoli the President's forces attacked those owing allegiance to Karami.

All efforts to halt the Tripoli fighting failed, with things made worse by the bitter antagonisms built up on each side. A typical incident came in the first week of September, when a lorry carrying a group of workmen from Tripoli was stopped by an unexpected Christian road-block on the way into the city. The men's identity cards were scrutinized and, when all of them were found to be Moslems, they were lined up; then a fourteen-year-old boy walked along behind them, shooting them all dead with a long burst from his M16. His reason: his brother had been killed the previous evening in fighting between Tripoli and Zghorta.

So desperate did the situation become that the Karami Cabinet was finally persuaded to use the Army to try to separate the combatants. Several factors made this possible in Tripoli, while it was still considered too risky in Beirut. The first was that the highly partisan General Ghanem had gone, and had been replaced by General Hanna Said. He was of course a Maronite, but was thought to be less committed to the Right-wing than his predecessor, though events were to show otherwise. Again, the lines in Tripoli were further apart and more clear cut, so that it was physically possible for the Army to interpose itself. And thirdly, it was believed that agreement between the President and the Prime Minister to bring the fighting to an end would ensure the obedience of the militia commanders on the ground. On all three counts the calculations were wrong. General Said was to align himself firmly with the Right when the final partition of the country came, the militias in Zghorta and Tripoli took no notice at all of the instructions of their political leaders, and the Army found it very difficult indeed to move between the battle lines. Then, five days after being ordered to take action, the Army further damaged its own credibility when one of its units got into a fight with supporters of Farouk Mokaddem, the Left-wing leader in Tripoli and Mr Karami's rival. It was Mokaddem's men who opened fire first, the Army claimed, though at the end twelve of the militiamen were killed and there were no Army casualties.

As the incidents increased in Tripoli and the Army was clearly unable to contain the situation, the futility of trying to use troops to stop the fighting became clear, and Karami's stubborn refusal to bring them into Beirut was shown to have been correct. Yet from the Right-wing point of view Army involvement was useful, for around Tripoli the result forecast by the Phalangists took place – the soldiers did join the Christian side. This further embittered the Left, which not only continued the fight whenever it found an opportunity around Tripoli but also saw to it that the battles spread to Beirut and were continued in Zahle. In the capital, the situation was made worse by the armed depradations which took place every night. Gangs of robbers, always carrying Kalashnikovs and sometimes with machine-guns or rocket launchers, systematically pillaged the smart shops of the centre of the city. The Sûrêté and Police Judiciaire, which were still functioning after a fashion, could do nothing about these large-scale thefts, and the Internal Security Forces were not prepared to get into a shoot-out with such formidable bands of brigands. So one by one, or more often half a dozen at a time, the shops around Hamra were cleared of their goods, with the merchants using the mornings to clear their stocks to safer places whenever it was possible to go out. A dusk-to-dawn curfew was announced by Chafic Haidar, the Governor of Beirut, in mid-September, but as no-one but the fighters of either side were ever on the streets after dark this was just one more empty gesture, and was in fact accompanied by an upsurge in fighting in which a cheap hotel in the Place des Martyrs collapsed after being hit by mortars. At least eighteen people, mostly Egyptians and Iraqis, were buried in the rubble.

So bad was the situation that Syria decided to take a direct hand in matters and for the first time dispatched the Foreign Minister, Abdel Halim Khaddam, to see if he could arrange a truce. With him went General Hikmat Chehabi, the Chief of Staff of the Syrian Army. The Syrians were plainly hinting that if the advice of their Foreign Minister was not taken then other means were available to restore order in Lebanon. With this implied threat there was also a conciliatory move, as the Damascus Government announced that the P.L.A. battalion which had been sent to Tripoli had been withdrawn. Khaddam stayed in Lebanon for a week and in that time managed the apparently impossible: he persuaded Kamal Jumblatt and Pierre Gemayel to sit together on a new body, the Committee of National Reconciliation, and at the same time arranged a ceasefire. Both these achievements seemed prodigious as they were announced, but they were short-lived triumphs. Jumblatt and his allies maintained that the first task of the new committee would have to be consideration of their reform programme, the blueprint they had drawn up for a radical overhaul of the National Covenant and the machinery of the State to allow much greater participation by Moslems. The Rightwingers, for their part, insisted that the first priority had to be the restoration of law and order, and said that no dialogue could take place while the violence went on. Since much of the fighting was being done by the Christian militiamen, this was obviously a recipe for indefinite postponement of any discussion. Soon both points became academic as the fragile truce was broken once again: this time because a workman employed by the Water Board, a Christian, was killed by a sniper while he was repairing pipes in a Moslem area. In the conditioned response of the mindless, Christian militiamen at a road-block sought victims on which to take their revenge. Three Druze were the first Moslems to come past and were shot out of hand in the callous retaliation which had become the norm. The direct and predictable consequence of both these acts was that the battles started again, and in Beirut they spread from the down-town commercial district and port to the centre of the city, engulfing the hotel area and the residential quarters in which most foreigners lived, as well as getting close to many of the Embassies. In the Bekaa Valley, the Christian militiamen of Zahle raided surrounding Moslem villages, apparently aiming to take the pressure off their comrades in the capital. The unexpected result was the dispatch of the Yarmouk Brigade of the P.L.A. from Syria to rescue the hard-pressed Moslems and the first open Israeli warning that it would intervene if Syria sought to take control of any part of Lebanon. At the same time, the Great Powers and Western Europe at last awoke to the possibility that the Lebanese civil war could lead to a general Middle East conflagration, if left unchecked. 'Serious expressions of concern' came from Washington and a few guarded comments about 'Zionist-Imperialist conspiracies' from Moscow, while the Europeans wrung their hands and urged someone – anyone except themselves – to do something to stop the bloodshed. The only ones who might have succeeded in doing so were the Arabs and, as usual, they were hopelessly divided. A meeting of the Arab League at Foreign Minister level was called in Cairo, but, as it was called by Kuwait at the open behest of Saudi Arabia, it was obvious that the aim was merely to enable two conservative Arab régimes to intervene in support of the Christians and thus to balance the influence of Syria and other radical countries on the Palestinian side. Seeing what was going on, Syria and the P.L.O. both refused to take part in the meeting, which achieved nothing at all. In Lebanon itself, meanwhile, President Franjieh was being blamed for the continuation of the fighting. His old colleague Saeb Salam joined with the dissident Maronite leader Raymond Edde to call for his resignation, and Rashid Karami made it plain that he considered the intransigence of the President and the direct involvement of the Interior Minister as the main stumbling blocks to any settlement – Camille Chamoun's militiamen were heavily engaged in the fighting on all fronts. Karami made several attempts to have Parliament convened, but on each occasion it was impossible to find a quorum, often because mortars began falling near the parliament building, or because armed men occupied the square outside and began gun battles with the guards.

As the fighting went on, there was an air of near-desperation as the few remaining uninvolved politicians – Karami, Edde, Salam, Ghassan Tueni, the outspoken and highly political publisher of *An Nahar* newspaper, Adel Osseiran, a leading Beirut Deputy, and a few others – searched for some way to stop the holocaust. The need grew hourly more urgent: on 8 October more than fifty people were killed when a rocket ploughed into a queue outside a baker's shop on Corniche Mazraa, and on the same day five children were hit by a stray mortar bomb. Such incidents occurred daily, killing innocent people on both sides indiscriminately, while totally failing to lead to any heart-searching or attempts to achieve a peaceful settlement on the part of the fighters; rather their thoughts always seemed to turn to revenge – following the Phalangist bombardment of the *souks*, for instance, in which Moslem shop-owners suffered the most damage, a band of Left-wing and Palestinian guerrillas staged a raid on Souk Tawile, a narrow enclosed street of fashionable dress-shops, jewellers and boutiques. In an orgy of wanton destruction every store was smashed, burnt and dynamited; no attempt was made to loot anything, for this was strictly a punitive affair, vandalism on a grand scale.

With the failure of the Khaddam mission in spite of its promising start, the Damascus Government was becoming increasingly concerned at the continuation of the violence and the very real danger that it would spill over from Lebanon or would involve Israel, with the certainty that, if that happened, a war for which the Syrians were not prepared would be bound to follow. So President Assad summoned Mr Karami and Yasser Arafat to Damascus, and in the first indication of the way his mind was working this normally quiet and reserved Arab leader pounded the table and shouted as he blamed the Palestinians for all that was happening in Lebanon. 'If only you had had more sense in the past...' he shouted at Arafat. His fit of despairing temper over, Assad got down to discussing possible ways of resolving the crisis, and the result was that Karami and Arafat returned to Beirut to make new efforts to get a truce. They were briefly successful, and on the morning of 11 October there were remarkable scenes in the streets as barricades came down and men who had been shooting at each other hours before kissed and hugged, and stuck flowers in their rifles. Amin Gemayel, the Phalangist military leader and son of the party founder, was escorted by P.A.S.C. men through Palestinian areas, and for once it seemed that a real truce had been achieved. Within hours, however, everything was back to 'normal': there was a report, true or false, no-one ever bothered to find out, that a Phalangist representative had not returned from a discussion with the Palestinians. Instantly the barricades were re-erected and the shooting began again.

At the end of October, Karami made one last attempt to exert his personal influence and authority. He persuaded Kamal Assad, the Speaker, to make one more effort to convene Parliament and reluctantly Assad did so. On the morning of 25 October, twenty-five Deputies managed to get to the Parliament building, a pleasant old Ottoman *serail* near the front line in the commercial sector of the city. The twenty-five men present did not form a quorum, but they could discuss matters among themselves and communicate the mood of the people to the leaders there. Others outside realized this and did not like even this informal exchange of views, so the Speaker soon received a telephoned warning that the building was about to be attacked. He, in turn, got in touch with Camille Chamoun, the Interior Minister, who was staying with Franjieh in the Presidential Palace at Baabda above Beirut. Assad asked for protection for the Deputies, a prime consideration in any democracy; Chamoun replied brusquely that there were not sufficient forces available to defend Parliament and advised the Deputies to disperse. They did so, perhaps with a clearer picture than before of the difficulties facing the Prime Minister on whom so many hopes were being pinned.

Karami himself was bitter and pessimistic. He realized there was little hope, but he was determined to have one more try; in a move reminiscent of the hunger strike of the Imam Moussa Sad'r, the Prime Minister went to the Parliament building and announced that he would stay there until the politicians he had called on to join him in seeking a solution arrived to offer their help, or until a way out was found. Arafat and a number of Palestinian leaders did call to promise their support, and from Damascus Abdel Halim Khaddam pledged any help Syria could give. So Karami came up with yet another peace-making body, this time called the Higher Co-ordination Committee, and succeeded in getting representatives of the Left and Right, and of the Palestinians and the Security Forces, to agree to serve on it. On this occasion Karami was helped by his timing and by the elements; it was the end of the month, so a truce was needed to allow money to be taken out of banks (if the militiamen were not paid, they would not fight next month) and there was the first solid downpour of rain of the winter. For a few days, it looked as though Karami's final attempt to stave off complete disintegration might have succeeded.

6

A way of
life and death

An eight-week break in the summer of 1975 and a series of scattered 'peaceful' days in the autumn of that year were in fact the only result of Karami's desperate attempts to end the conflict. In July and August there seemed to be a genuine attempt by all sides to come to terms, but the brief periods of calm in November were no more than breathing spells to allow the combatants to rest and bring up new supplies. The war had taken hold now, it had become a way of life – or death – and people had difficulty in remembering what it was like without the constant sound of gunfire, the search for food, the automatic choice of sheltered routes whenever anyone ventured out, the swift identification of 'incoming' and 'outgoing'. Not that a few people did not still try to bring things to an end: Rashid Karami, above all, never gave up; there were others, too, and outstanding among these was Sharif Akhaoui, a middle-aged, bald, diminutive radio announcer, who became the one voice of sanity and honesty in Lebanon throughout this desperate year.

Sharif Akhaoui was a continuity announcer and producer of Radio Lebanon who early in 1975 conceived the idea of a daily rush-hour programme warning drivers of traffic jams, road hazards and so on. His programme was an instant success, for he mixed a lot of personal comment with his facts: he noted that road improvements already approved and for which the money had been allocated had not yet been started, and named the officials to blame; he gave the times that Directors arrived at their Ministries, or recalled politicians' promises which had not been kept. Akhaoui brought a breath of life and sense to a radio station noted previously only for its sycophantic reporting of the doings of the so-called great of

ABOVE LEFT Few of the traditional leaders of the country were able to hold on to their positions during the war; Saeb Salam, a former Prime Minister whose support came from the Sunni population of West Beirut, was one who worked hard to do so, though with indifferent success.

ABOVE RIGHT The Maronite Church was deeply involved in the conflict—at times, monks took up arms to defend their monasteries, while Father Charbel Kassis, their leader, was one of the main advisers to the Phalangists.

RIGHT Yasser Arafat, the commando chieftain who had to spend as much time on politics and diplomacy as he did on the conduct of the battle.

LEFT Rashid Karami was a Prime Minister without power for most of the civil war.

BELOW The one politician who maintained and enhanced his position was Sheikh Pierre Gemayel, head of the Phalangist Party and of the Right-wing coalition.

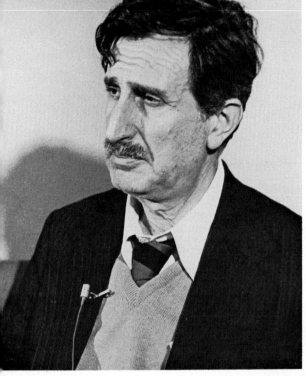

LEFT The Left-wing bloc was led by the unlikeliest figure of them all—Kamal Jumblatt, millionaire landowner, Socialist, and head of the strange Druze sect.

BELOW In Beirut, much of the fighting was done by the Mourabitoun, the little-known independent Nasserite organization. Their chief, Ibrahim Kleilat, was transformed from a back-street gangster into a politician by events.

ABOVE Camille Chamoun, President during the 1958 war, shared the leadership of the Right during the new conflict.

LEFT Elias Sarkis, the quiet civil servant, was the Syrians' choice as new President of the embattled country.

BELOW When Suleiman Franjieh was elected in 1970, Pierre Gemayel's vote was vital, but by 1976 the alliance became strained as Franjieh refused to relinquish office.

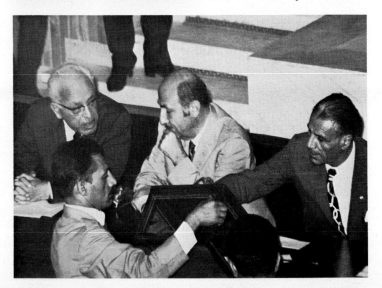

ABOVE Kamal Jumblatt found himself increasingly isolated as the Palestinians took over the fighting, and so tried to form his own Fakhreddin Army, a very mixed force made up entirely of his own Druze supporters.

BELOW Franjieh started his six-year term of office with a visit to Cairo to receive the seal of President Nasser's approval. Its benefit was short-lived.

ABOVE The political decisions which ended the war were taken at the mini-summit in Riyadh, and as a symbol of their new-found agreement, old enemies happily posed together, (*left to right*): King Khaled of Saudi Arabia, Elias Sarkis of Lebanon, President Sadat of Egypt, President Assad of Syria, Crown Prince Fah'd of Saudi Arabia and Yasser Arafat, the Palestinian leader.

LEFT The street fighting was bitter and at close quarters. Here, two Right-wing militiamen check a former Leftist strong-point.
ABOVE Behind a barrier of Christian-owned warehouses, Tal Zaatar burns as Right-wing gunners pour in more fire from an adapted Russian anti-aircraft gun.

ABOVE The Holiday Inn (*right*) was fought over for months as the battle of Kantari brought the war to the centre of Beirut. This hotel and the Phoenicia behind it were destroyed before the Left-wing finally forced the Phalangist defenders out.

BELOW The RPG (rocket propelled grenade) was one of the most frequently used weapons. It is on the end of the launcher held by the masked gunman, while the second man holds a Kalashnikov, the universal weapon of the Palestinians and Leftists.

ABOVE Amid the devastation, life had to go on. But the toys were guns borrowed from bigger brothers; the folding-stock version of the Kalashnikov held by the three-year-old was no imitation.

BELOW Syrian Foreign Minister Abdel Halim Khaddam (*right*) spent weeks trying to negotiate an end to the war, and several times reached agreement. Seen here with Rashid Karami, he is celebrating one more ceasefire; in the end, it was Syrian tanks, not Syrian diplomacy, which stopped the battles.

the country. And when the war began, Akhaoui extended his service: he arranged a special office for himself at the head-quarters of the Internal Security Forces and broadcast direct from there. No matter how bad the fighting, he always managed to reach the microphone and usually contrived to make a personal reconnaissance of the worst trouble spots before going on the air. Soon Akhaoui was the one man trusted in Lebanon. In the early days optimistic government state-ments, written by civil servants the previous evening, would be broadcast each morning, asking people to go back to work. Immediately, Akhaoui would come on to tell everyone to stay at home. 'You would be mad to go out,' he would say. 'The gunmen are everywhere, every street is dangerous.' And it was Akhaoui the people listened to, not the suspect voice of official-dom. Nor did Akhaoui spare any side; himself a Shia, he regu-larly castigated the 'madmen' of Left and Right, sometimes get-ting so worked up by a particular incident that he was almost screaming abuse on the radio. Yet his advice must have saved hundreds of lives, for as his fame grew so did his sources of information, with people telephoning him within minutes of an incident, so that he was able to pin-point new road-blocks being established and to advise people how to avoid them; he identified areas being strafed before the Internal Security Forces knew which targets were being attacked, and his voice was often more effective than the most complicated negotiations in securing the return of hostages.

At the beginning of November, Akhaoui's influence was at its peak, and he used it in a remarkable way to demonstrate the popular will and to show the politicians and the militia leaders that the people had had enough. Akhaoui called for 'a march for peace', and thousands of people responded. Shia, Sunni, Druze, Maronites and Greek Orthodox went out into the streets to demonstrate their hatred of violence; led by priests, sheikhs and imams, the peace marchers brushed aside gunmen who tried to stop them; from the church towers the bells rang out, calling this time not for help for a beleaguered Christian enclave but for the rescue of a nation; and from the minarets, the muezzins chanted verses from the *Koran* calling for tolerance, understanding and peace between brothers. It was a spontaneous demonstration of the popular will, but it

91

was not enough. The marchers, courageous though they were, could not penetrate the no-man's-land between the opposing sides, braving the constant hail of bullets there. They had to confine themselves to comparatively stable areas of the city, so that their message was seen only by those already in sympathy. Not that the gunmen would have taken any notice, for attitudes were so hardened that only the victory of one side or the other, or a peace imposed from outside, had any hope of stopping the carnage.

A 'good' day in Beirut now was one in which a housewife could slip out for half an hour to find one of the itinerant vegetable sellers who still plied their trade, collecting their goods on the outskirts of the town where the farmers from the South delivered it, and trundling their barrows miles to their favourite pitches, then often having to shelter to escape a local battle before being able to sell their wares. Prices, of course, were increased three or four times; still, it was a hazardous occupation for meagre returns. In Hamra, once the chic main street, stalls of every description lined the pavements and all the shops were closed; in Raouche, too, once the fashionable residential quarter where embassies were housed and diplomats lived, the shop-keepers driven out of the *souks* set up their stores; Beirut had become a makeshift city, its people living from hand to mouth in constant danger, services non-existent and civilization gone. Beirut Airport was still open, the one lifeline to the world of sanity outside. Only M.E.A. was still flying in and out, and the hard-pressed crews were working hours I.A.T.A. would never have sanctioned as they flew their planes to Amman, Athens or Nicosia at the end of a long trip to 'tanker' fuel back to Beirut for the next day's flights; nothing was getting through from the refinery at Tripoli in North Lebanon, the only source of aviation fuel in the country.

Outside Beirut, things were just as bad. The private war between the Moslems of Tripoli and the Christians of Zghorta continued, while in the Bekaa Zahle was besieged by hundreds of Palestinians reinforced by P.L.A. units from Syria. Isolated Maronite villages tried to conclude local deals for 'protection' with Palestinians in their area. In just the same way, residents in the cities hired their own gunmen to protect their homes: the going rate was L.L.250 a month, about £50. The guard supplied their own arms and ammunition. The Army went to the aid of the people of Zahle, holding off the strongest attacks, a move which was seen as further evidence of Army partiality, but one which was in fact quite proper, for if this pleasant resort town had been overrun there would have been thousands of casualties.

Throughout Lebanon there now came another change: in the past, everyone had carried his identity card with him, for it always had to be produced going through road-blocks, shown to the police, or displayed when visiting government departments. Now the I.D. cards were torn up, for they showed a person's religion; and on the basis of that small piece of paper, hundreds had already lost their lives, murdered for a faith they might hardly believe in, but which was recorded against their name for all time. Foreigners, too, had to make their dispositions: no-one carried more than a small amount of cash, and expensive watches or important documents were always left behind, for robbery was rife and armed hold-ups took place at any time of the day or night.

In this lull in the storm of war, a cursory stock-taking was possible and the results were announced by the Chamber of Commerce: 2,500 businesses burnt, damaged or looted, and damage estimated at £1,800 million had been caused. There was time, too, for a few humanitarian – perhaps theatrical – moves. Hearing of the plight of the people of the Jewish quarter of Beirut, who were sheltering in two of the synagogues in Wadi Abou Jamil and were desperately short of food and water, Yasser Arafat sent a special group of his men to their rescue. It was an area very close to the front line, under regular mortar bombardment and with snipers able to pick off anyone moving about. Yet the carefully chosen group of el Fatah men put down their arms to take in lorry-loads of supplies, and of course made sure that a group of photographers accompanied them. Even in the midst of war, Arafat was not the man to let a propaganda opportunity pass.

In Tripoli, an uneasy stalemate had developed; in Zahle, both sides had decided to give themselves a break; and in Beirut too, there was little activity – the 'hotels front' was the most active, with the Leftists holding the Palm Beach and Excelsior, and occasionally trading fire with the Phalangists in the

Holiday Inn, St Georges and Phoenicia. As the Right-wing redoubts were almost cut off and could not be supplied, at the beginning of December the Phalangists pulled out of these positions, leaving the front line a little further to the east. So much easier had the situation become, in fact, that the recently formed Armoured Strike Force of the Army, a mobile unit intended to be rushed to trouble-spots and to contain flare-ups in the fighting as they occurred, felt able to show itself. At the same time the people venturing out of their homes for the first time in weeks realized very well that this was no more than a lull and also that both sides were using it to re-supply their forces and to prepare for the next upsurge. This was made obvious with reports of a ship laden with arms arriving in Jounieh Bay, in the solidly Christian-dominated area north of Beirut. Karami was determined to show his authority 'even if it means exploding the whole situation', so he sent officers of the Security Forces to examine the ship's cargo. They blandly reported that it was not carrying any war-like material. So sure was the Prime Minister that it was, that he dispatched another larger and more carefully chosen unit of the Security Forces to Jounieh to conduct a thorough search. Now the partisan nature of the Presidency came into the open again; Franjieh countermanded Karami's order, strong units of the Phalangist militia sealed off Tabarja Beach, where the vessel was unloading, and prevented the Security Forces from getting anywhere near. The man in charge of the operation: Tony Franjieh, the President's son. Gemayel admitted that arms were being brought in and claimed, probably correctly, that six shipments for the Left had arrived in Sidon in the previous seven days. 'We pay a lot of money for our arms, which we buy with great difficulty,' he said. 'Others get them free and with ease. Arms are entering this country from all areas and being distributed to all sides. It is not possible to let arms flow to one side and deny them to the other. Forbidding a party arms to defend itself in such a situation is tyranny, and totally unacceptable.'

At this half-way point in the war, the Palestinians were still getting the bulk of their supplies overland from Syria, along the Arafat Trail; Iraq also sent arms overland in lorries, while Libya, and to a lesser extent Algeria, shipped material in through Sidon. Many of the consignments were earmarked by the donors for the particular groups which they sponsored: Iraq had to look after the Arab Liberation Front, its commando group in the same way that Saiqa belonged to Syria; it also sent supplies to the other bodies in the 'Rejection Front', which were also supported by Libya. This was not always easy, for Fatah was still the main guerrilla organization, needed the most arms, and had the most muscle to see that it got them. There were frequent arguments about supplies and, later, a dispute was even to lead to violence in Sidon, though in general the flow was so great that there was enough and to spare for everyone, including the Lebanese Left-wing forces led by Jumblatt.

On the Right, as Gemayel said, there were greater difficulties. When the Phalangists and the N.L.P. first began building up their militias in the early 1970s, they relied largely on rich Lebanese emigrés to help them, usually through the Maronite-dominated World Lebanese Cultural Union, the 'club' to which most people of Lebanese descent living outside the country belonged. The arms bought on the comparatively open market came mainly from Eastern Europe, such traditional dealers as Czechoslovakia or Rumania. Later, even millionaires found it impossible to provide the funds needed and governments quietly stepped in. Saudi Arabia was among the donors, Egypt gave some help, and so did Jordan. Later it was the Americans, through the C.I.A. regional centre in Athens, which began giving clandestine assistance; and the C.I.A. arranged the first meetings in Cyprus between Phalangist representatives and officers of the Israeli Intelligence Service. As a result of these meetings, held in an obscure hotel in the Troodos Mountains, Israel began sending regular arms shipments to Tabarja Beach, the small, isolated cove just above Jounieh which was used to discharge all weapons. The arms themselves were bought from Spain, Portugal and Belgium, and it was the Left which suddenly began experiencing difficulties in getting supplies, as Israel mounted a naval blockade of Sidon. Russia, though willing to send material, would not risk an incident by using one of its own ships, so that Libya soon became the only major practical source left to the Palestinians.

In December 1975, those problems were still in the future. The Palestinians believed they were winning and were eager to resume the battle; the Phalangists thought they had been held back by their leaders still looking for a political solution, and were as keen as their opponents to go back to war. Not that there was total peace, merely what passed for calm in Lebanon. Thus traffic began flowing again in the main areas of the capital during the day, about thirty per cent of undamaged shops opened, and efforts were made to persuade the itinerant traders to move out of Hamra to allow the big stores there to resume business. At the same time, intermittent fighting went on between Chiah and Ain Rumaneh in the suburbs, in Sinn el Fil and Nabaa, between Kahhaleh and Aley in the mountains, in Zahle, and on the outskirts of Tripoli and Zghorta. Peace of a strange kind. Yet there were hopes that it could be extended, and these centred mainly on a visit to be made to Damascus by Pierre Gemayel. The invitation from President Assad had come after efforts at mediation by M. Couve de Murville, the French Foreign Minister, and at a time when the leaders of the main Right-wing party seemed ready for compromise; it seemed to offer a good chance for the beginning of a real dialogue between the warring factions. This was clearly the view of the small minority on both sides who wanted the war to go on, for there was a series of incidents which exacerbated the tensions between the two sides: a lorry-load of *Korans* was destroyed, churches were vandalized, and stray acts of violence threatened to start a new conflagration, while artillery duels between Kahhaleh and Aley, started by the Palestinians, threatened the opening of a new theatre of operations in the mountains above Beirut, until now fairly quiet, apart from the main Beirut–Damascus highway which had always been a confrontation line.

So it was against the usual background of anarchy that Gemayel and his Phalangist lieutenants flew by helicopter from Jounieh to Damascus – the road was too dangerous for them to go that way. There were high hopes for their mission, dashed before the negotiators had even reached the Syrian capital, for about that time the bodies of four men were found murdered on the outskirts of the Christian village of Fanar in the Phalangist-dominated Metn district. All were Maronites and, without waiting to see who the culprits were or what had led to the killings, the Phalangists immediately began to seek revenge. Road-blocks were erected in every Right-wing-held area around Beirut, and Phalangist and N.L.P. militiamen stopped everyone who came along. The Moslems among them were killed on the spot; according to reports at the time, more than one hundred men were summarily executed in retaliation for the murder of the four Maronites on what became known as 'Black Saturday'. In fact, later investigations showed that 370 people were killed on that day – fifteen every hour, one every four minutes, and all on the basis of the word opposite the section marked 'confession' on an identity card. It was the men trying to keep the port working who suffered most; stevedores, Customs men, tally clerks and all the other petty officials needed were picked up in the first sweep by the Rightist militias, and almost all died as the Christians vented their artificially induced rage on a section of the population which had voluntarily chosen to continue working in a Rightist-held district, and was made up mainly of the poorest sections of the population who had played no part in the fighting and were more concerned with scratching a living than pursuing an ideology. The abductions and killings spread to every area around Beirut, and continued the next day as the battle-fronts exploded in a new blaze of rage. Camille Chamoun, whose men had played a major part in the butchery, cynically used the savage events of Black Saturday and his position as Minister of the Interior to call once more for the direct use of the Army, whose involvement was still one of the main Right-wing aims. The Moslem leaders would naturally have nothing to do with such a proposition, and were fully occupied in trying to protect the Christian minorities living in Moslem-held territories – it was a time when anyone with the 'wrong' religion stayed very close to home and tried to enlist the help of friends in one of the armed groups around. In general, the leaders were successful in preventing any sort of retaliation of the same kind as that carried out by the Right, but they could not stop a new punitive assault launched against the Phalangist militiamen holding the so-called District Four, the hotel area of Kantari and Minet el Hosn. Ibrahim Kleilat's Mourabitoun began the assault, spurred on by their determination to exact vengeance for what had happened over the previous two days, and were successful in throwing the Phalangist defenders out of the St Georges and Phoenicia hotels, causing considerable casualties to the defenders: at least thirty-eight of the hotel's Christian employees were massacred at the Phoenicia. There were ugly scenes which were to be repeated time and again as the Mourabitoun hitched the body of one Phalangist fighter to a jeep, and towed it triumphantly and obscenely through the streets. The Mourabitoun also launched an attack on the Phalangist headquarters itself in Sioufi, and for a time looked as if they might take this psychologically vital objective. So great was the danger that the Phalangists would be completely overrun that a strike force of the Army was used to try to stop the battle, but the soldiers had to be withdrawn when they appeared to be acting completely on behalf of the Right-wing forces – not this time because they wanted to, but because the Mourabitoun were on the attack and the Phalangists being driven back. The attackers could not break through the last Phalangist defence line near their headquarters, however, and after more than a week the battle ground to a halt as the Left-wing militia realized they had taken all the ground they could, and stood no chance of scoring the outright victory they had sought. They had made gains and might have made the final breakthrough, if they had been given total support by the Palestinians; but Yasser Arafat was under heavy pressure from Syria not to go too far. The Syrians wanted a negotiated peace which would maintain much of the old balance in Lebanon, and would not accept outright domination of the Right by the Left. The Syrians, it seemed, were not the committed, dedicated supporters of the Palestinians and the Left that they had always appeared in the past; both sides in the war suddenly had to stop and take stock of an apparently new situation, though in fact there had been no change in President Assad's policy: it was merely that force of circumstances was making him tip his hand rather earlier than he might otherwise have done.

The bitterness caused by Black Saturday and its aftermath did not disappear as the fighting slackened on the main fronts. Rather it had become a fact of life, so that Christian and Moslem militiamen lived with a deeply nurtured hatred; there could be no going back, and there was precious little hope of repeating the scenes of the past when the fighters came out of their gun emplacements to embrace and swear friendship. The iron had bitten deeper than ever, and compromise no longer seemed possible. Certainly this was realized on the Right, for now came the beginning of the policy of clearing the predominantly Christian areas of their minorities. Antelias, a few miles north of Beirut, a Moslem enclave, was attacked a few days before Christmas, a number of people killed, and the non-Christian families living there forced out, to make their painful way to the Moslem districts of West Beirut in a pattern that was to become familiar. A Shia village nearby was treated the same way, and all over the Metn and Kesrouan those living in Moslem communities were driven away. Faced with what they were coming to see as the possibility of defeat in Beirut, the Phalangists were preparing for the ultimate retreat into a redoubt of their own, the Christian heartland of Mount Lebanon. For the first time, there was open talk of the partition of this tiny state, 3,400 square miles in a coastal strip never more than thirty-five miles wide and one hundred and thirty miles long.

Officially, the Right denied any idea of splitting the country, though it was increasingly clear that this was in their minds, because of all the continued attempts to regain lost territory. In counter-attacks on the outskirts of Beirut the Phalangists made some headway, while in the city the Army went into action against the Palestinians, forcing them out of the St Georges and Alcazar Hotels, though these were re-occupied as soon as the soldiers pulled out. In Tripoli the fighting went on as steadily as it did in the capital, with both sides using tanks and armoured cars either seized from the Army or given away by their crews, who often continued to man them — earlier, the Phalangists had demonstrated their ingenuity by manufacturing their own armoured vehicles from steel plating mounted on a lorry chassis. Just before this sorry Christmas in Lebanon, Rashid Karami paid another visit to Damascus in an effort to reach some sort of understanding with President Assad, the one man capable of restoring order. The story of the Lebanese Premier's trip was a fair reflection of the chaos in the country and the ordinary physical difficulties faced by those trying to find a solution, let alone the political ones. First

Karami's motorcade was shot up on the way out of Beirut, then he was held up at a road-block, and finally two of the vehicles travelling with him were commandeered. On the way back, the party was stopped by the fighting around Zahle and found it impossible to move along the main road to Beirut. The Prime Minister had to make an ignominious return to Damascus to ask for help in getting back to his home. He was eventually taken to Beirut in a Syrian Air Force plane.

In Lebanon, both Moslem and Christian festivals were always public holidays, and in happier times Christians would give their Moslem friends presents at Id al Fit'r, and Moslems would return the compliment at Christmas. This year, there was none of that: the Patriarch, Antonius Khreish, decreed that there should be no celebrations, only prayers for peace. It was unnecessary advice, for no celebration was possible. The shooting went on in the suburbs and in the commercial areas of Beirut, in Tripoli and in Zahle, still besieged by Palestinian troops. All but basic foods were scarce. If the church bells had been rung, it would have been taken as an alarm call, and there were no shops selling the luxury gifts the Lebanese had previously delighted in buying. In the past, Hamra had always been festooned with lights, with loudspeakers blaring out carols continuously; now, this main street of the capital city was closed and shuttered, with vegetable sellers and drink stalls on the pavements for a few hours in the morning if things were reasonably calm. On Christmas Day, some local dispute led to shooting in Hamra itself, so that even the stall-holders gave up and went home. And in the two days between Christmas and the twenty-second ceasefire of the civil war which was announced on the 27th, more than two hundred people were kidnapped, many never to be seen again, and forty were killed.

Beirut, which had always recovered so quickly from past disasters, now showed no signs of even attempting to return to normality when the fighting entered one of its periodic lulls. Most foreign firms had pulled out, so that only a few expatriates were left clearing up their affairs in what had been the most cosmopolitan city of the Middle East. Even U.N.W.R.A., which in theory should still have been needed and which was staffed mainly by Arabs, announced that it too was going. At the Post Office thirty million letters shipped in during the early months of the year were lying undelivered, while in the port warehouses full of goods of all kinds regularly went up in smoke because phosphorus bombs were being used in the mortars as well as the ordinary explosive charges. And it was not only the 'regular' fighting which the bemused and battered citizens of the country had to face: the general state of lawlessness was getting worse, as convicted prisoners were freed by one party or another. In the first days of 1976 the notorious Sands Prison in Beirut was attacked and its inmates freed – a foreigner serving time for drug offences refused to go out into the dangerous streets and had to be rescued by his consul the next day. In Baalbeck and Tripoli, too, criminals were released and immediately went back to their old methods of earning a living, safer than ever before, as killing was now an officially sanctioned occupation and no penalties followed: when a man was arrested by police in Aley for murdering two Christians, seventy people besieged the police station until he was released.

Yet, as the year began, Karami the eternal optimist kept radiating hope and talked of the re-establishment of order. Looters would be 'attacked unmercifully' he said, and asked people to go back to work at the same time that the radio was speaking of fighting throughout the country and warning that all roads were unsafe. The Prime Minister's intentions were good, but more and more he was out of touch with the reality imposed by the warring parties. On the Christian side there was an increasingly clear idea of what should be done: in private, and occasionally in public, such powerful opinion-makers as Father Charbel Kassis or Father Paul Naaman were speaking of 'the Christian heartland' and the need to clear 'foreigners and alien elements from the homeland'. The Phalangist leaders understood the message and on 4 January 1976 took another practical step towards clearing their area of any outside presence: a blockade of the Tal Zaatar refugee camp was begun. This camp was one of the biggest around Beirut, in an area surrounded by Christian-owned factories and workshops which had once supplied some sixty per cent of Lebanese industrial output. It had been established when the first wave of Palestinians reached Lebanon and had grown over the years, with the commandoes at times forcing the poor

Lebanese out of the high-rise apartment buildings on the periphery of the camp. Now some 30,000 Palestinians lived there, 'an alien enclave' totally surrounded by Christian areas, and frequently trading fire with them. The official Phalangist reason for beginning the blockade was that the Palestinians in the camp had been attacking neighbouring Dekwaneh and other Christian suburbs, which was certainly true, though who began the regular hostilities was in doubt; in fact, the Right thought they could starve the Palestinians out without too much bother and so save themselves trouble and casualties. In an effort to restore its credibility with the Left, the Army went into action and tried to escort a dozen flour lorries from West Beirut into Tal Zaatar. The Right-wing militiamen, mainly from Camille Chamoun's N.L.P., opened fire on the soldiers in their fairly vulnerable armoured personnel carriers, and the convoy had to turn back. The Christians had shown they meant to maintain the blockade.

As fighting went on around Tal Zaatar, with the 1,500 Palestinian commandoes inside the camp trying to battle their way out to link up with another relief column on its way from Beirut, the Palestinians sought to create a diversion which would allow them to relieve the pressure on Tal Zaatar. They chose to open a new front south of Beirut, at Damour, for two reasons: the first was that it was one of the strongholds of Camille Chamoun and a base for his party; the second was that, as long as this Christian bastion remained untouched, there was the possibility of 'a stab in the back' attack from the South. The Palestinians feared a Christian presence in their areas almost as much as the Christians feared the Moslem enclaves in theirs. So the Palestinians began shelling Damour and the neighbouring Christian villages of Mishref and Jiyyeh, to be answered by immediate Christian attacks on the camp of Dbayyeh, north of Beirut, which was inhabited mainly by Christian Palestinian refugees. After two days the camp was overrun and, though some fifty-odd people were killed after resistance had ended, the Phalangist militiamen were reasonably restrained in their treatment of the Palestinians there largely because they were Christians. Still, some 2,500 of them were made refugees all over again, though a number of others were allowed to remain once the commandoes had been winkled out and stayed there throughout the war, under the watchful eye of Phalangist guards. To make up for this defeat, the Palestinians stepped up their attacks south of Beirut; Chamoun, who had been staying with Franjieh in the Presidential Palace at Baabda, flew by helicopter to be with his people in Damour and, as his nearby residence became a refuge for thousands of Christians from surrounding villages, he sent an urgent request to Franjieh for help from the Army. General Hanna Said, the new Commander, ordered one relief column to set off from Sidon and another from Beirut, and in the meantime sent the Lebanese Air Force into action. Rashid Karami, who was Minister of Defence as well as Prime Minister, knew nothing of this until he saw three Hawker Hunters strafing Palestinian positions around Damour and anti-aircraft gun emplacements in Sabra and Chatila camps near the international airport, which had been closed when the fighting moved to Khalde. Karami was at the home of Sheikh Hassan Khaled, the Mufti, seeking his support for a new appeal to the Palestinians to halt their attacks as the jets went in; he immediately telephoned General Said to find out on whose authority the air strike had been ordered. Told that the Palace had asked for it to be carried out, Karami tried to have it called off, pleading that civilians were being hit. He was ignored. Another who saw the strikes was the Syrian Chief of Staff, General Hikmat Chehabi, who was at the Presidential Palace at Baabda where he had been trying to arrange yet another ceasefire. As he watched the Hunters go in, the General told his aides to pack up and call his helicopter to take them all back to Damascus. 'Clearly, my mission has been overtaken,' he told President Franjieh.

This time, however, the Palestinians were prepared for the air attacks. They had learnt the lessons of 1973 in a way the Army had not intended. On this occasion there were no Palestinian concentrations to strike, only widely dispersed, well-camouflaged and well-sited positions. And the fighter pilots had to be a lot more careful than they had been on that earlier occasion, when the only opposition they had experienced had been wild and merely morale-raising small arms fire. This time, the Palestinians had Sam 7s, the Russian-made, hand-carried surface to air missiles which homed in on the heat of a plane's exhaust. The Palestinians scored no hits, but the knowledge of these weapons made the pilots a lot more careful, and a lot less accurate.

The Palestinians had another advantage they had lacked before: they had been equipped with a new communications system, and had also captured or been given some of the radio-transmitter sets used by the Lebanese Army. Signallers from the regular forces were among those who had defected to the Left, so that the Palestinians were able to listen in on the Army network. The result was that they knew of the dispatch of the relief columns to Damour and were able to engage them at places of their choice; one of the Army task forces was pinned down, the other badly mauled and forced to retire, and the fate of Damour was sealed. Yet there was still a chance: the Right-wing forces decided to do as the Palestinians had done in the first place, to create a diversion, so they put in a strong attack on the slum areas of Karantina and Maslakh, at the northern entrance to Beirut. First there was a savage mortar bombardment of these pitiful shanty towns, inhabited by the poorest of the poor – so abject was the obvious poverty of Karantina that a previous government had surrounded it by a high wall to prevent it offending the eyes of motorists passing by on their way to the North. As the barrage of bombs fell on Karantina and Maslakh, the Palestinians pressed their attack on Damour, where Chamoun had been forced to retire to his home at Saadiyat, a little further south. Once again, the country was in flames; and once again Karami tried to shock people into appreciating the seriousness of the situation by offering his own resignation, citing the 'mutiny' by the Army command as his excuse – General Said's refusal to stop the use of the Air Force. It had no effect at all. The rival offensives continued, with neither side making any move to relieve their besieged comrades, merely pressing on towards their own objectives. In the Bekaa the Left began a siege of two Christian villages; in Damour the last pockets of resistance were being reduced, while the main Palestinian force engaged the Army column at Khalde, near the vital international communications centre of Radio Orient, at the edge of the airport; to the north of Beirut the Phalangists systematically reduced Karantina and Maslakh, and on 19 January took these two Moslem areas in an orgy of bloodshed. Dozens of men, women and children were killed as the militiamen stormed in; hundreds more afterwards. The Phalangists, most of them wearing ostentatious crosses around their necks, separated the men from the women and children, marched them a little way off, and shot them. Christian women from nearby districts watched the whole grisly scene, laughing and joking, and shouting encouragement to the executioners. Then Maslakh, the slaughterhouse district, was set ablaze; and at Karantina, the area in which people and animals were held in quarantine in earlier times, the bulldozers were brought in, and every dwelling was razed, with what contents were considered not to be worth looting. Soon the area was flattened.

Revenge came instantly. On the following day the Leftist forces stormed into Damour. There was not the same indiscriminate killing that had gone on in Karantina or Maslakh, though there certainly were summary executions and some very nasty individual cases of mutilation and torture: half a dozen scalps lay in a gutter after the attackers had swept through the town. That was followed by an orgy of wilful destruction in a deliberate policy of an eye for an eye: the houses of Damour were not the corrugated iron and breeze block affairs which were the best in the Moslem areas; these were substantial stone-built dwellings, reflecting the reasonable prosperity of the farmers of Damour, the main market garden for Beirut. Every house was systematically pillaged, then burnt or blown up.

At Saadiyat, Chamoun's home, 5,000 refugees milled about, guarded by a small squad of Army commandoes. Chamoun himself contemptuously rejected a propaganda-inspired offer of safe conduct and 'rescue' made by Arafat, but he was whisked out by Army helicopter as soon as the evacuation of his people by dozens of fishing boats had begun. A notable feature was that the Palestinian and Leftist forces did not press their attack on Saadiyat while Chamoun was there, as they could easily have done; Jumblatt gave the order to hold back, though Chamoun's pleasant house was razed as soon as he left it. Jumblatt and Chamoun had been bitter enemies since 1958, but had been reconciled only a few months earlier, and the Druze leader still believed that it might be possible to reach a negotiated peace.

It was a hope which had to be abandoned within days as the last vestiges of authority in the country crumbled away. In Christian areas, police stations and army posts were taken over by the militias in protest against the lack of help to the Maronites of Damour; in the rest of the country, Moslem forces seized key positions in readiness for new attacks, while the Army began to break up, with whole units declaring for one side or the other, and taking all their equipment with them. But in the Bekaa, there was a sudden restoration of order: the Yarmouk Brigade of the P.L.A. began pouring across the border, and this time the Palestinian soldiers were not being sent to the aid of the commandoes in Lebanon. Units fanned out to all parts of the country, and to Beirut, as more and more men were committed.

Syria had finally decided to intervene.

7

Politics and personalities

The first Syrian intervention was a mild affair compared with what came later, and at first it was highly successful, as it was accepted by all parties. It came at a time when Palestinian victories enabled the Left to be magnanimous, while the prospect of total defeat made the Right eager for compromise. Not that the Syrians appeared to care, for they sent the Yarmouk Brigade of the P.L.A. – a much reinforced Brigade with some two hundred tanks – rolling into Lebanon the day before Abdel Halim Khaddam, the Syrian Foreign Minister, arrived at the Presidential Palace at Baabda accompanied by General Chehabi and General Naji Jamil, the Air Force Commander. It was on 20 January, while the Palestinians and a militia led by Mustapha Sa'ad, son of the Sidon mayor killed when the war started, were storming Damour and the Phalangist bulldozers were erasing the last traces of occupation at Karantina, that the Syrians arrived to deliver their ultimatum; and the composition of this three-man delegation was intended, and taken, as a clear indication of what would happen if President Assad's orders were not obeyed. It was obvious, too, that no outside power would try to stop the Syrians, who had made careful international preparations. Only a week before there had been strong warnings against any intervention in Lebanon, and America had laid down that neither Syria nor Israel should interfere; now there was a welcome in Washington for firm Syrian action, and Dr Kissinger described the role of Damascus as 'statesmanlike'. Israel, too, had promised it would react strongly to any Syrian troop movement, but now carefully pointed out that Palestinian forces were being used, not Syrian, and thus saw no need for any response. This remarkable Israeli *volte-face* had been arranged by America, which approved the Syrian action in advance; King Hussein was the intermediary and the Saudi Arabians had also played a part, following King Khaled's visit to Damascus at the beginning of January. The only man to be strongly and publicly opposed to the arrival of the Syrian-sponsored troops was Camille Chamoun, bitter at the loss of Damour and incensed at the lack of world sympathy for the massacre there in which at least forty-seven civilians were killed. Chamoun found himself on his own; Pierre Gemayel, who on 7 January had said his militia would fight to the last man if Syrian troops invaded Lebanon, now welcomed the Syrian initiative. He had received private assurances from Damascus that the P.L.A. would not be sent in to side with the Palestinian commandoes but to restore order and police a truce, and so firm were the promises given that Gemayel was prepared to take a chance. On this occasion, he was a great deal more far-sighted than most of his colleagues.

As the P.L.A. battalions moved across the border from Syria with their armoured vehicles, artillery and, above all, the full support of the Syrian Army, the fighting in Lebanon gradually died away, as it seemed that the Palestinians had a firm grip on the largest portion of the country, while the Christian Right had effectively cleared all but two of the Moslem enclaves in their area and had a defensible heartland which was also beginning to prove that it could exist economically. The Syrians were careful to show that they meant to be even-handed in their approach, so their first move was to relieve the Moslem pressure on a number of Christian villages. Units were also sent to the Palestinian-controlled areas of towns and cities, particularly Beirut, to form joint patrols with P.A.S.C. and with the Lebanese Security Forces, where they were still functioning, to restore order. In these districts, the Syrian-backed forces exhibited no partiality towards their Palestinian brothers-in-arms: on dozens of occasions commandoes who were stopped at road-blocks had their weapons taken from them and smashed; ten looters were shot; and the 'police' patrols tried unsuccessfully to halt the ransacking of Spinneys, Beirut's biggest department store. There was one happy moment during this episode when a well-dressed, obviously prosperous man staggered out of the building with two sacks filled with all the most expensive and exotic foods he could grab – to find his Mercedes had been stolen while he was inside.

The main force used by the Syrians in this first effort to re-store sanity to Lebanon was the crack regiment of the P.L.A.; the Yarmouk Brigade was probably the best unit of Palestinian forces in existence: it had fought in Jordan in 1970, in Lebanon several times after that, and beside the Syrian troops on the Golan Heights in 1973. It was to all intents and purposes a regular part of the Syrian Army, with Syrian officers, though most of the other ranks were Palestinians. This was not enough to make the Brigade side with the commandoes, so in an effort to balance the situation Arafat quietly arranged for the Ain Jalloud Brigade of the P.L.A. to be sent from Egypt, and units of the Quadissiyah Brigade from Iraq; but for all their pro-testations of friendship, neither Egypt nor Iraq were over-keen to help the Palestinians publicly at this time, and only small numbers of troops were dispatched. Iraq was later to send regular soldiers to fight on the side of the Left-wing forces in Lebanon, and the P.L.A. men they did move in quickly went over to the Palestinian side once the full-scale Syrian invasion came; but, presented with what appeared to be a Syrian *fait accompli*, Sidam Hussein and the rulers in Baghdad were reluctant to become involved so far from home. With good military sense they made their contribution by mobilizing forces on their border with Syria, causing a large part of the Syrian reserves to be diverted there.

Egypt's policy was more complicated, particularly as it was Egypt which was largely responsible for Syria's actions. It was the September agreement between Israel and Egypt, negoti-ated by Dr Kissinger, which finally pushed Syria into a complete re-examination of its role and policies, and an even-tual change of direction, though such a shift had been brewing for some time. The Syrians were convinced that Egypt under President Anwar Sadat intended to abandon the military option, and to throw in its lot with the West. Desperate politi-cal efforts were made to avoid this in the year preceding the signing of the Sinai Agreement, but the Egyptians would not change course; the galloping birth rate, still running at over three per cent in spite of all the efforts made to curb the pop-ulation, the huge waste of desperately needed resources on defence, and the increasing expectations of the people, which had to be satisfied if the régime was to survive, all pushed President Sadat in one direction. He had to rely on the Americans to bail him out, for the Russians certainly would not, and to get the help of the United States he had to pay the price: Sadat had to take the first step along the path marked out by Dr Kissinger, which meant a formal agreement with Israel and thus a near-explicit declaration that Egypt did not intend to launch a new Middle East war or to join in one if it could possibly avoid it.

The effect on Syria was immense. President Hafez Assad, the quiet professional soldier who had succeeded in welding the country together after twenty politicians had failed in as many years, suddenly found himself isolated. He knew better than most that Syria could not go to war with Israel on its own; but he had land he needed to get back just as much as the Egyptians wanted the return of their lost territory. The Golan Plateau was not merely a bare and desolate terrain to be fought over, it was also the site of one major town and a number of large villages, as well as an important agricultural region. To the Israelis the plateau was desperately important because it kept Syrian artillerymen away from the Heights, the Golan cliffs overlooking Lake Tiberias and the fertile plain around it, from which they could make life near-unbearable for the farmers for twenty miles around. The Israelis had no intention of negotiating the return to Syria of the Golan Plateau, particularly when President Assad was so clearly in a position of weakness, with his ally Egypt lost to him. Under American pressure, Israel was reluctantly ready to make a small 'cosmetic' adjustment to the ceasefire line, but in return wanted the repopulation of Kuneitra, the main town, so that thousands of civilians could act as a trip-wire on behalf of Israel for any renewed Syrian attack. Assad could not agree to this without himself agreeing to abandon the possibility of war or the hope of regaining all the area lost in 1973 and 1967, a move which would have cost him the confidence and support of his hard-line Army and Party advisers.

So Assad set about building a new northern alliance which would pose a just-credible threat to Israel, and so enable him to negotiate from a position of greater strength. His first move was to arrange a *rapprochement* with King Hussein, a remarkable feat showing the determined pragmatism of both leaders, for only five years earlier Syrian tanks had rolled into Jordan and come close to putting an end to the Hashemite Dynasty. Assad himself had been largely responsible for foiling that adventure by Saleh Jadid, who was then the leading figure in the Syrian Ba'ath Party, and so he had a basis on which to make his overtures to the King, while Hussein was as alone and isolated as Syria, suffering the same loss of credibility as a result of what was generally seen as the Egyptian defection; he was also smarting from the decision of the latest Arab Summit Conference, which had recognized the P.L.O. as the sole representative of the Palestinians on the West Bank of the Jordan, an area which had been Jordanian since 1950 and which Hussein still saw as part of his kingdom. Hussein and Assad got on very well together, not only because of their common interests in getting back their conquered territories but also because, for all their very different backgrounds, both were trained career soldiers, great survivors who were up against very hard times. So the Syrian President from a small and poor 'heretic' Moslem sect which had its sole base in the northern mountains of Syria concluded a formal alliance with Hussein, the hereditary monarch and descendant of the family of the Prophet. Self-interest in both cases had driven them towards each other, yet once in contact they discovered they spoke the same language and took a similar cynical view of politics.

Assad's next need was to expand his new alliance, and to do so he turned to the Palestinians. Syria had always been the main supporter of the Resistance Movement, not only for ideological and patriotic motives but also because of geographic propinquity. The vast bulk of Palestinian arms and supplies had to be shipped in through Syria, no matter who the donors were, and there had been many occasions in the past when Syria had reminded Arafat and his lieutenants of the situation by holding up shipments to register disapproval of some action. For Assad had a very low opinion of the Palestinians; he was himself a professional, an airman who had known no life outside the military from his boyhood. All his training and his personal thinking made him sceptical of the ability of guerrilla forces to make any impression on Israel. He saw the Palestinians' need to put on a show, to demonstrate their determination to return to their homeland, while refusing to admit that they could achieve that without the aid of Arab armies, particularly his own. Assad firmly believed that the Palestinians were already in Syria's debt and would be to an ever-increasing degree; so he saw no reason why Syria should not become the Palestinians' overlord, in the same way that the Syrians had made Saiqa their fifth column within the Movement. This organization had been created with the intention of making it the most formidable and most militarily powerful section of the Resistance Movement, and at the outbreak of the Lebanese war it was the strongest fighting force the commandoes had. Only Yasser Arafat's determination had prevented Saiqa from taking over the whole movement, and his insistence on keeping Fatah as a combat unit as well as a political party eventually allowed the Palestinians to mobilize and to expel Saiqa.

To create the sort of bloc he wanted, Assad had to be in command and he could not allow a situation in which the Palestinian tail was able to wag the Syrian dog: Arafat and Fatah had to be brought under Syrian domination – once that was achieved, everything else would follow naturally. The outbreak of the war in Lebanon complicated Assad's plans. He had been quietly working through Saiqa to gain control of the Resistance, but the war united the Palestinians and made it impossible to pursue that course. So Assad at first tried to exert his authority by continuing to act as the Palestinians' quartermaster, while giving them the advice and help he thought would best suit his purposes. This did not work either, for the Palestinians have always been a stubbornly individual people and they did not intend to alter in the midst of a war not of their seeking. Their early successes made them even more intransigent and Assad more apprehensive. There was a real possibility of a new order in Lebanon in which the Palestinians would at worst have a major say and at most could even be the dominant factor. If the latter happened, Lebanon would quickly become 'a confrontation state' rather than the neutral enclave it had always sought to be, and the Palestinians would soon provide Israel with an excuse for some major preventive measure. Syria would then face the prospect of being drawn into a war for which it was not ready at a time it had not chosen; it would also be forced to spread its forces more thinly on the ground, for a government in Lebanon dominated by the Palestinians and the Left would give Israel a ready excuse to send its troops on a flanking move into Syria by way of the Arkoub and the foothills of Mount Hermon. That could have happened in the past, but Lebanon's special position and its international support had prevented it; there would be no such restraints in the future.

What Assad would have liked to see was the continuation of the old order in Lebanon, with a few changes designed not only to satisfy his own and his people's genuine support of their form of socialism and Ba'athism, but also to ensure a situation in Lebanon free of the antagonisms and violence of the past. It would not suit Syria to have either the Left or the Right in undisputed control; rather Syria wanted a situation of reasonable stability in which the régime in Damascus would exercise direct authority over the Palestinians, and use them as the third pillar of the bloc being built up. The hope was that at some time in the future the old enemy Iraq would change or be changed enough to be brought in as well, and then there would indeed be a powerful group of which Israel would have to take notice.

There were one or two quiet private reasons guiding Assad's Lebanon–Palestinian policy as well. Firstly, the President's brother, Rifaat Assad, was particularly friendly with Tony Franjieh, the son of the Maronite Lebanese President. Both were of a kind; they liked fast cars and all that went with them, easy money and an easy life. Both, too, combined this with the military prowess for which people from the mountains seem to be renowned. For all their playboy image, each of them was as at home with a gun in his hand as with a handful of chips at a gaming table. The young Franjieh was the leader of the Zghorta Liberation Army, the fiercely dedicated and extremist militia he had formed in his own home town; and Rifaat Assad, as a Colonel in the Syrian Army, commanded the Special Forces, the picked troops always stationed near Damascus, which were, in effect, the Republican Guard of the Syrian Ba'ath Party and of President Assad in particular.

On the negative side, Assad also had a particular antipathy towards the leaders of the Palestinian Revolution. He did not like Arafat, and he did not like the way the Palestinians seemed to court publicity. He was a man who believed in deeds and was unimpressed by the rhetoric and propaganda which were the staples of the commandoes. Equally, on hard political grounds, he was influenced by the undemanding support given to the Palestinians by Iraq and Libya, two brother Arab nations for whom the Syrians entertained no brotherly feelings at all.

So the Syrian troops were sent in to Lebanon. Though the nucleus was the Yarmouk Brigade, several thousand regular Syrian soldiers suddenly found themselves volunteering for this Palestinian unit. The invaders seized the vital crossroads at Chtaura from which columns could be sent north to Zahle and Baalbeck, west to Beirut, or south to Marjayoun and across the Anti-Lebanon range to Jezzin, Sidon or Tripoli. On the border bridgeheads were established, and tanks and guns were dug in to control the whole Bekaa Valley. Small units were sent off to Beirut and other towns, and nearly one hundred Syrian officers were selected as 'truce supervisors', though in effect they were military administrators, passing on the orders of Damascus. A Joint Military Committee was formed to police the truce, with representatives of the Syrians, Lebanese and Palestinians; it was significant, however, that the Palestinian representatives were Zuheir Mohsen, head of Saiqa, and Colonel Saad al Sayl of the Yarmouk Brigade. Still, this twenty-sixth ceasefire of the civil war appeared to be holding in a way that none of the others had done, and the Syrians carefully radiated confidence about it all, even when bullets hit the car carrying Khaddam and Karami to Baabda. Zuheir Mohsen proclaimed: 'The civil war is over, and I don't believe anyone will be able to start it again.' In the main towns, traffic cautiously reappeared on the streets, though nightfall was still the signal for all but the men with guns to huddle at home; the banks at least talked of re-opening, food was easier to find, and in general things did look better than at any other time in the previous year.

Yet, for all the hesitant attempts to bring the country back to life, the process of disintegration was still in force. Most serious of all, the Army was now breaking up; Lieutenant Ahmed Khatib, a young Moslem officer frequently passed over for promotion, led a breakaway movement in the Bekaa and proclaimed himself head of the 'Lebanese Arab Army'. Whole garrisons and barracks followed his lead, arresting Christian commanders and replacing them with Moslems; at least forty tank crews defected to this new Moslem Army with their vehicles. At the same time, Christian units sided openly with the Right, so that the long-feared split in the Army, avoided in 1958, took place in 1976. The first result of this break-up of the sole remaining functioning institution of the State was the *de facto* partition of the country. As long as the Army had existed as the nominal arm of the Government, lip-service could be paid to the idea of unity and there would have been something to build on in the future, as there had been in 1958. Now there was nothing: the gendarmerie followed the example of the Army, and split in much the same way; the police simply disappeared. Yet the Syrian-imposed peace created the climate in which reconciliation seemed possible, particularly as Khaddam and his aides emphasized their commitment to a reform of the Lebanese system. They were not there merely to impose a ceasefire, they said, but to lend their good offices in finding a lasting solution which would satisfy the natural aspirations of the Left, while protecting the legitimate interests of the Christians; this was a tall order, and one which they singularly failed to achieve.

At first all went well. Franjieh was summoned to Damascus and, when he baulked because, he said, of the danger that his entourage might be ambushed by Khatib's men on the way through the Bekaa, the Syrians promised him protection, and made it very plain that when they whistled he had to obey. At the meeting between the Syrian and Lebanese Presidents, Assad promised he would restrain the commandoes in return for a commitment to reform from Franjieh: if the Right made concessions towards the Moslems and the Left, then Syria would see that the Palestinians obeyed the provisions of the Cairo Agreement. Franjieh did not like it, but he had to do as he was told. So on 14 February he went on radio and television to announce a new seventeen-point 'programme of national reform'. It was a curious document which tried to satisfy all parties to the conflict in the country, and naturally ended by pleasing none. The main objection of the Left was the provision that the President should continue to be a Maronite, with a Sunni Prime Minister and Shia speaker. This endorsement of the traditional practice seemed to Kamal Jumblatt's Progressives and even to the old-guard Moslem leaders to be enshrining for all time the confessional nature of the Lebanese system; they were not mollified by the plan to divide Parliamentary seats equally between Christians and Moslems, for they understood the Lebanese scene better than the Syrians and they realized very well that real power lay with those who could dispense maximum patronage – the top men – rather than with parliamentary democracy. The Right, for their part, did not like the idea of free compulsory education, which would benefit Moslems much more than Christians, nor did they approve the move towards abolition of confessional appointments to civil service posts. Even the powerful Lebanese Press objected, for there was an ominous paragraph dealing with the newspapers: 'Responsible freedom of the Press shall be guaranteed, in conformity with social policy and to promote national unity, and to strengthen Lebanon's Arab and international relations.' The Lebanese newspaper editors, the last champions of free writing and informed argument in the Arab world in spite of their corruptability, knew that this meant just one thing: censorship. The Palestinians were the unhappiest of all: they were winning the war, they were sure, and now they were being stopped by the people who had always been their staunchest supporters; something was going badly wrong, though they could not see quite what. The parts of the proposed new National Covenant which applied to them were bad enough, and showed the extent of Syrian capitulation to Right-wing fears, in the view of the commandoes. Under the *pax Syriana*, all Palestinian camps around Beirut would be de-militarized and all heavy weapons would be removed; there would be no return to Karantina, with its strategic position controlling the main highway from Beirut to Tripoli; and the provisions of the Cairo Agreement would be strictly enforced, plus all the other niggling restrictions which the Lebanese had been able to add over the years.

At least the Syrians had managed to create a climate in

which people were arguing about the proposals rather than shooting each other in support of one view or another; and there were traffic jams in the streets, the banks opened for the first time in two months, while the airport was operating more normally than it had done since well before the previous Christmas. There was time, too, to take stock: at least 12,000 killed in the first year of the war, 40,000 wounded, 180,000 people displaced; about twenty per cent of the dwellings in Beirut had been completely or partly destroyed; more than half the factories had been damaged, burned or looted. Yet these statistics did not lead to a determination to avoid further violence; rather they gave rise to enhanced bitterness between the various communities and a new determination to exact vengeance.

It was the members of the more extreme organizations in Lebanon who felt most affronted by the Syrian peace formula, for they got nothing out of it: not even the system of proportional representation in Parliament suggested a year before by Jumblatt, which would have given them some chance of direct participation in affairs, was approved by Damascus. And as even the most moderate Moslem leaders, such as Saeb Salam, came out in opposition to the new National Covenant, largely because it barred Moslems from the Presidency, the extremists felt able to begin the fighting once again. The general situation made this all too easy. After an early burst of activity, the P.L.A. was showing itself no more able to put an end to the lawlessness in the country than the regular police had been or the Palestinians themselves. Robberies, murders and kidnappings were commonplace. To get any attention at all theft in Lebanon had to be on a huge scale: it was only the rifling of the headquarters of the British Bank of the Middle East in Bab Idriss which was noted, and that not for the mere L.L.10 million in cash which was taken (£2,000,000) but for the clearing out of the bank's safe deposit boxes. It was in these privately owned boxes that the owners of shops in the gold *souks* had deposited their treasures when they rescued them with Army help five months earlier; other wealthy Lebanese had chosen this respected, sound foreign bank as the repository of their own jewellery, bearer bonds and so on. No-one was ever able to work out exactly how much was stolen, but conservative estimates were that goods worth L.L.50 million

(£10 million) were taken in addition to the money, a haul which makes the Great Train Robbery look an amateurish effort.

The chaotic everyday existence provided the conditions in which intermittent hostilities could go on, though it was the Lebanese Arab Army and all the other defections from the Security Forces which brought about the new crisis. Rashid Karami was supposed to enlarge his six-man Cabinet to provide an administration capable of putting into effect the Syrian reform proposals promulgated by President Franjieh, but the Prime Minister found himself bogged down in his efforts to get normal life working again, with every proposal he made opposed by one side or the other. The case of the deserters was typical, though it also formed the main stumbling block to effective action. Jumblatt wanted the Moslems who had set up their own forces re-integrated into the Army; the Right, including General Hanna Said, the Army Commander, would not hear of this, and demanded that the men should be court-martialled or at least quietly expelled from the Forces. The real difficulty was that it was all an academic exercise, as there was no authority capable of bringing Khatib or anyone else to justice without starting the war all over again, particularly as Khatib had identified himself closely with the Left and was one of the few who had publicly condemned the suggested new National Covenant: 'It does not provide a fundamental solution to the Lebanese crisis,' he said, 'and the minor reforms it proposes are not commensurate with the sacrifice that has been made. In any case, the civil war is not over as neither side has achieved what it wanted.' The young Lieutenant Khatib, passed over for promotion for eleven years and by his own admission no intellectual, had a much clearer grasp of the situation than Zuheir Mohsen or any of the other leaders.

8

The bloodiest battles

Far from coming to an end, the war was in fact reaching a climax. The pause which followed Franjieh's broadcast of the 'reform programme' in February was short-lived, and no progress at all was made in forming a new Cabinet which would put the proposals into effect. Karami, as usual, was bogged down in the day-to-day routine of trying to contain the proliferating incidents or to bring together rival politicians, and had neither the time nor the power to institute the wide-ranging changes envisaged in the Syrian-inspired formula for a new order in Lebanon. Throughout the country the slightest spark could ignite a region and frequently did: in Qubeiyat, a northern village, for instance, a car was ambushed and two men in it killed. Almost certainly this was part of a local vendetta which may well have had its origins generations earlier – such things were common in the remote Akkar region. Instead of being added to the tally of victims of the feud to be avenged by a similar exaction of blood over the years, the incident led to a mini-war between neighbouring Christian and Moslem townships, with mortars and machine guns used on both sides; the Lebanese could no longer afford the luxury of settling matters by recourse to a gun without risking a general conflagration.

The biggest problem facing the Government now was not the security situation, bad though this was; rather it was the existence of the Lebanese Arab Army and the daily defections to it which were taking place. Even in areas untouched by the fighting, soldiers were choosing which side they preferred, so that the regular Lebanese Army itself was left as a rump force consisting mainly of headquarters' staff. At Rachaya, the vital crossroads town controlling the route from Syria to the South, the three-hundred-strong garrison arrested the Christian

119

colonel in charge and declared itself for Ahmed Khatib; in the South, the area headquarters at Marjayoun followed the example of the High Command and remained neutral, while the garrison at Tyre, which controlled the border area from Ras Nakoura to Bint Jbeil, went over to the Arab Army. More ominous still, there were signs that the malaise was spreading to the Air Force, always a strongly Christian arm of the Forces largely because its technical role called for the higher educational standards which the Christians usually possessed. Colonel George Ghoraieb, the Air Force Commander, called for political reforms throughout the country and an amnesty for deserters, while at the Army headquarters at Yarze 250 junior officers held a noisy meeting and demanded the 'restructuring' of the Army. General Said finally bowed to pressure and declared an amnesty for everyone who had left his post, deserted, or joined any breakaway unit; but it was too late, and this pardon came from the wrong man. The General had ignored the orders of Karami, the Defence Minister, while carrying out the request of Chamoun, the most militant of the Right-wing leaders; and he was seen too much in the company of Gemayel. General Said had lost the confidence of the Moslems just as surely as his predecessor.

The swift fragmentation of the Army was matched by the final breakdown of law and order throughout the country. An average of thirty major crimes were being reported each week, while casual murders and robberies were so common as to pass unremarked. The simmering war was being used as an excuse to settle old scores and any man with a gun – and there were few without one – considered armed robbery a proper way of earning a living. At the same time, sudden flare-ups of violence came as vivid reminders that no solution to the long-standing ills of the country had yet been found. In Tripoli, the confrontation with the Zghorta Liberation Army was still going on; in Zahle, Christians and Palestinians faced each other and there were daily skirmishes or exchanges of fire; in Beirut, the veneer of normality was paper thin, and time after time life came to a standstill again as a flurry of shots signalled a new outbreak of violence. At the end of the first week in March the situation was as bad as it had ever been with kidnappings and killings making life impossible once again. All the old remedies had been tried and had failed, so now some of the moderate leaders of Fatah got together with the senior officers of the Beirut Army garrison and came up with a new idea, which they hoped might lead to the re-establishment of a unified army under middle-of-the-road Moslem leadership. They sent messages to General Said and obtained his tacit support for what was proposed. On 11 March the plan went into effect: a group of P.A.S.C. men escorted the Garrison Commander, Brigadier Aziz Ahdab, to the radio and television station in the heart of Beirut, close to the hotel area where sporadic fighting was still going on. Brigadier Ahdab made his broadcast, declared that he was taking over, called on President Franjieh to resign, and said a new government would be formed within a week. If this had been a real coup, the tanks should have been rolling through the streets, picked men would have been occupying key positions around the town, and others would have been arresting the representatives of the former government. But this was not serious; it was a televised attempt to put pressure on the President and to provide a new focal point around which the Army could rally and re-unite. There was no follow-up to the announcement that the Beirut garrison was taking over, no move towards imposing control, no deployment of troops – not least because the Army forces in Beirut commanded by Ahdab were far inferior in numbers or equipment to the Palestinians by whom they were surrounded or to the Praetorian guard which the President had available at his Baabda palace.

Ahdab was a strange man who mixed a deep love of publicity and personal advancement with a genuine wish to do something to extricate Lebanon from the morass into which it was sinking. He was a mixed-up man: during his strategy-planning sessions with Palestinians, he refused to remove his American training certificates and honorary membership badges of various U.S. police forces and army units from the walls of his office. He had a habit of playing with the pistol he always wore and, when asked about a special fitment on it, explained that it was a silencer so that he would not disturb people if he had to shoot at night. Brigadier Ahdab tried to do it all by television, a medium of which he seemed particularly fond and which he soon learnt to exploit; he quickly understood camera angles and lighting, and made sure he was shown to best advantage. This was his only accomplishment: after his initial announcement, he went on the air several more times to announce the formation of a military command council, to warn the President that force would be used if he did not obey the demand for his resignation, and to call for an end to the fighting which was still going on.

None of this had any effect at all. Franjieh ignored the whole thing and never even acknowledged that a move against him had been made. In Beirut, the fighting intensified, and around the country the skirmishing went on. Lieutenant Khatib and his Army made no move to join Ahdab, but instead went ahead with their own plans. The Brigadier's move had failed. It was a bold effort and might have succeeded if it had been given more open backing by the Palestinians, who privately encouraged this attempted television take-over. The motives were mainly good, while the execution was hopeless. Whatever the textbooks say, command of a television station alone is not enough; some forces capable of taking real action have to be deployed and Brigadier Ahdab had none available. His action served to crystallize the situation, however, so that the Members of Parliament felt able to convene formally and to pass a motion calling for Franjieh's resignation. He had said he would consider stepping down if two-thirds of the Deputies called on him to do so, and on this occasion sixty out of the ninety-nine did so; several Deputies admitted later that they thought they were voting for a *fait accompli*, not having realized that the Ahdab coup was a shadow on a screen rather than a sword at the throat of the régime. It made no difference: Franjieh announced that he was going to stay on no matter what the vote; so Khatib now had one of the strongest military groups in the country with tanks, armoured cars and artillery, though his direct control was minimal, as each unit formed an autonomous group which took orders from no-one. One of the most important of these units was commanded by Major Yakoub Daher; its strength lay in its possession of a number of pieces of field artillery. And now Major Daher also decided that President Franjieh should go; he had the means, he thought, to make him do so, though he did not have the backing of the Palestinians or the control of any mass medium which would allow him to put his message over. Still, he had the guns and he had a working arrangement with the commander of another unit stationed on the Damascus highway near Sofar; so Major Daher and his colleague began a pincer movement towards the President's Palace at Baabda, Daher's group moving along the coast road from Sidon to Beirut ready to strike up into the hills, and the second column advancing down the main road leading through Sofar to Bhamdoun and Baabda.

These twin thrusts provoked the turning point of the war. They forced President Assad to declare himself openly, to show that he was no longer on the side of the Palestinians and that he was quite prepared to move against them. As the group attacking along the Damascus–Beirut road reached Sofar, they found their way barred by a strong force of the Palestine Liberation Army with tanks dug in beside the road, guns on the surrounding hills, and troops quite ready to give battle. Major Daher himself found his advance blocked by Saiqa. These Syrian-backed Palestinians had anti-tank weapons set up at Khalde ready to stop Daher's armoured personnel carriers and guns, and warned him they would open fire if he attempted to push through. Both columns of the Lebanese Arab Army wisely refused to offer battle, and stopped half a mile away from the forces sent to halt them. This still left Daher in a position from which he could shell the President's Palace, only five direct miles from Baabda, so he deployed his guns and on 23 March began a bombardment of the Palace.

This was no sudden act of aggression, for the Palestinians and their allies had launched a new offensive three days earlier following the failure of Syrian attempts to control events in Lebanon. Lieutenant Khatib had been summoned to Damascus to be admonished for the moves 'his' forces were making against President Franjieh; then the conservative Moslem leaders, Karami, Salam and Assad, were called to Syria in their turn to be given new instructions. Men of one of the extremist groups making up the Rejection Front were determined to frustrate this: as the three were boarding a Syrian Air Force jet at Beirut Airport a rocket was fired at the plane, which was hit and caught fire. Karami, Salam, Assad and their aides barely escaped with their lives. In the Chouf, Druze followers of Kamal Jumblatt fought Christians from Jezzin, and Jumblatt announced the formation of the 'Fakhreddin Army', an exclusively Druze force named after a seventeenth-century Lebanese hero-prince, a man who existed more in the Druze leader's fertile imagination than he did in fact. Faced with these new fronts and new political constraints, the Palestinians began an all-out attack on the Phalangist redoubt jutting into western Beirut, and in no more than twelve hours of combat they succeeded in taking the Holiday Inn, which had held out against desultory attacks for almost six months. The difference this time was that the Palestinians and Mourabitoun had Army units to lead the assault, and experienced Army officers to direct operations. Throughout the day, rockets and shells smashed into the building, delivered at almost point-blank range; a tank was firing from the intersection at Rue Clemenceau only five hundred yards away. As night fell tracer poured into the windows from which the defenders were still returning the fire, then under cover of armoured cars the Mourabitoun and the Palestinians stormed into the building, methodically clearing each of the twenty-six storeys in classic style, kicking open doors, tossing in grenades and spraying every open space with bullets before rushing in. Once all the Phalangists were killed, the victors happily posed for pictures in the hotel lobby, where the headless torso of one of the defenders still lay; other bodies were hitched to jeeps and dragged through the streets of the quarter in grisly proof of victory. It was this which brought the downfall of the Mourabitoun left on guard in the building during the night: a force of red-bereted men in P.A.S.C. uniforms arrived and brusquely ordered them out. The officer in charge shouted at them to form up in the courtyard and told them their behaviour had been a disgrace. As the Mourabitoun sheepishly formed up, the supposed P.A.S.C. men opened fire; they were Phalangists in disguise. They killed eighteen Mourabitoun and quickly brought up reinforcements to re-take two floors of the Holiday Inn; but they could not hold it, and next day they were wiped out by another assault led by armoured vehicles and a second attack by Palestinians still on the upper floors. This time the Inn was properly and effectively garrisoned, and ceased to be fought over, though it was frequently used as a sniper position by Palestinians or

Mourabitoun and made movement hazardous on the harbour road in East Beirut.

In swift reaction to the fall of this bastion of their salient in West Beirut, the Right-wing forces began a random bombardment, which was quickly returned. The first target of the Christian artillerymen stationed in the hills above Beirut was the Bain Militaire, where Lieutenant Khatib had established his headquarters. This building was on the sea-front, so that any shells which fell short smashed into a densely populated residential district, and the gunners preferred to err on the short side rather than over-shooting and letting their shells fall harmlessly into the sea. The barrage was accompanied by indiscriminate mortar bombing; neither side had any targets to aim at, but merely pumped in bombs in the rough direction of the enemy. This was a practice which was to continue on and off for months, and was one of the worst features of the war; those killed were invariably civilians and often it was children or women who suffered the most: the children because in the heat of a Beirut summer they had to go outside to play, and the women because they were the ones who had to queue for bread, vegetables and the other scarce necessities of life.

With the level of violence higher than ever before, the Cabinet finally met at Baabda to approve a Syrian plan to get rid of President Franjieh yet avoid for him the ignominy of having to resign before his term was up. The idea was that Parliament should pass a new law providing for a President to be elected within six months of the end of his predecessor's mandate; when this was done, the Syrians thought, Franjieh could gracefully step down and allow his successor to take over or at worst could work in partnership with a new Head of State. The Cabinet meeting was brief and formally approved the plan; it was obvious that the Ministers did not want to linger at Baabda, still a target for Major Daher's guns at Khalde, which in turn were being answered by Phalangist artillery stationed near Yarze. Government agreement to the Syrian idea seemed to spur the fighters on to greater efforts, perhaps because they feared that a genuine ceasefire might follow. Whatever the reason, the Left attacked the last Phalangist bulge in West Beirut with a new ferocity, and within days captured the Normandie Hotel, the Phoenicia and the unfinished Hilton. The partition of the capital was becoming a fact, just as the country was being divided.

Forced into the basement of his Palace by the repeated shelling from a section of the Army of which he was supposed to be Commander-in-Chief, Franjieh made a desperate appeal for help to Syria, which responded by an ostentatious movement of troops to the frontier and a summons to Jumblatt to present himself in Damascus. His reply: 'I am too busy directing the battle.' America gave implicit approval of any step Syria might decide to take – this time Kissinger called President Assad's approach 'constructive' – but nothing could be done to halt the steady bombardment of the Baabda Palace. So during the night of 25 March, the President, his family and his guards made a hurried and undignified exit. The dogs were left behind, with masses of clothes and personal belongings, though a tric-trac board – the backgammon of the Middle East of which Franjieh was a master – was taken as the President fled, a pistol stuck in his belt.

The abandonment of the Palace had no tactical or strategic importance, yet it was a tremendous boost to the Left, a signal defeat for the Right, and an important move in the *de facto* partition of the country. Gemayel summed up the situation in a near-desperate broadcast which seemed to be a last rallying call to arms for the Christians: 'Our people and our Army are dispersed, our institutions disintegrating and our land occupied,' he said. 'There is no legislature, no judiciary, no sovereignty, no security and no freedom. Ruin and destruction spread over villages and cities, towns and mountains. I appeal to you all, men and women, to unite for the homeland. Perform your holy duty of defending the homeland which faces disintegration.' The Phalangist leader was not overstating the case, for, in addition to their successes in Beirut, the Palestinians were also advancing in the mountains, long considered the inviolable Christian stronghold. The important towns of Ain Tourah and Bikfaya, Gemayel's birthplace, were threatened and a total Palestinian victory seemed possible.

The rank and file Palestinians were quite sure that nothing could now stop them, though their leaders were less confident. Arafat and his lieutenants took very seriously the Syrian moves, and began making preparations for an eventual con-

126

flict – an unthinkable idea to most Palestinians, for Syria had always been their ally, and it was Syria rather than Egypt which was admired for the part it had played in the 1973 war. Most Palestinians ignored the possibility of a direct Syrian intervention, believing that the possibility of an Israeli response would deter Damascus. Arafat was more realistic; he had read correctly the signs from Washington and the suddenly moderate Israeli statements. Syria could come in, he knew, and if it did so would certainly move against the Palestinians, not the Phalangists; precautions had to be taken, so quiet orders were given and Fatah units moved into position near every Saiqa office or strong-point. The attitude of Saiqa had long been suspect; now it was recognized as a potential fifth column, and the ambition of its leader Zuheir Mohsen to take over the whole movement was seen as a factor which had to be taken into account.

Arafat openly charged Syria with protecting the Lebanese President and with preventing the Left from carrying through its military campaign to a successful conclusion, which would end the fighting in the country. Yet Arafat and Jumblatt were both still prepared to compromise; Jumblatt, for all his inflammatory rhetoric, would still have settled for something very like the old Lebanon, so long as it was governed in accordance with his programme of relatively minor reforms aimed only at giving the Moslems of the country equal opportunities with the Christians. Arafat wanted an end to a war which was doing nothing but harm to the Palestinian cause and the return of conditions which would allow him to continue his basic struggle for the establishment of a State of Palestine. So the two men accepted a pressing invitation to visit Damascus, even though it came at a time when the fighting had reached a new peak and when Syria was clearly and obviously heavily involved through its control of the P.L.A. units in Lebanon. The summons to the Syrian capital came at a moment, too, which seemed highly suspicious to the two leaders of the Leftist forces: King Hussein had just been there for a meeting with President Assad, and they recalled that the last occasion on which the King had paid a visit was immediately followed by the dispatch of the P.L.A. to Lebanon. Still, the two men made the hazardous trip, leaving behind the full-scale battle in which the indiscriminate shelling of western Beirut by Christian artillerymen was being answered by a bombardment of Kahhaleh and other Right-wing strongholds by the Lebanese Arab Army guns at Khalde, with both sides regularly trading mortar fire. It was on 28 March that Jumblatt arrived in Damascus and immediately had a meeting with President Assad. That same evening the Syrian 'guard of honour' outside the villa put at Jumblatt's disposal was faced with a problem. Their guest suddenly appeared with his entourage, got quickly into his car and set off for an unknown destination. The puzzled guards had been told of no appointments and did not know where Jumblatt was going. They thought of stopping him, but decided against it and Jumblatt was able to drive unhindered back to his battle headquarters at Aley. He had decided to make his sudden and unannounced exit because he had learnt of a Syrian plan to bring him face to face in Damascus with the Phalangist 'Foreign Minister', the devious Karim Pakradouni, who had become totally committed to the Syrian viewpoint. Jumblatt feared that even a meeting with Pakradouni would be misunderstood by his supporters and allies or would dishearten his troops, and so pulled out of Damascus. Back in his own territory, he issued a calculatedly offensive statement: he thanked President Assad for his lunch and said he hoped to be able to invite the Syrian leaders to take lunch with him soon – in Bikfaya, Gemayel's home town.

Arafat, meanwhile, had stayed on in Damascus and, when he returned to Lebanon, sought to modify the uncompromising position of his Leftist allies. Arafat was all in favour of a truce; he was far more experienced than Jumblatt both in the art of survival-politics and in the conduct of military operations, and he had also been given the benefit of some more plain speaking by President Assad. In spite of all the successes chalked up by the Leftist alliance over the past weeks, he knew better than most that the tide could change and realized that, if too uncompromising a front was presented, the Syrians would not hesitate to move. So Arafat counselled caution and restraint, his two stock cards in any negotiations; this time neither Jumblatt nor the more extreme leaders such as Ibrahim Kleilat of the Mourabitoun would have anything to do with such a policy. As far as they were concerned, they were winning and they were determined to go on to the end. Nor would they take seriously the clear international signals which were being made; encouraged by Iraq, whose Ambassador braved the road to Aley for a meeting with Jumblatt and Kleilat, the Leftists pushed ahead with their military offensive.

On both sides it was the artillery which was the dominant factor now: Christian artillerymen loyal to Franjieh were in Kahhaleh, Broumanna and Fayyadiyah, so that they could shell both Aley and the Moslem areas of Beirut; Major Hussein Awad, commander of another column of the Lebanese Arab Army, sited his guns to return the fire and shell the Christian area of Hazmiyah, while both sides lobbed mortar bombs indiscriminately into the opposing areas. It was random terror which brought about the most complete shut-down of Beirut during the whole war; in Hamra, various pieces of a man killed by a mortar blast while he was crossing the road lay there for a day because no-one would venture out to move his remains, and even then a shoe with a foot still in it was missed and was only later kicked into the gutter. In Achrafiyah the mortaring cleared the streets and made it impossible for staff to get in or out of the main hospital, the Hôtel Dieu, while in the port area the Palestinians battled it out building by building with the Phalangists grimly defending the last approaches to their Sioufi headquarters.

So desperate was the situation that some form of outside intervention seemed bound to come: the only question was who would move first, though it seemed obvious that Syria had been given the green light by Washington. Dr Kissinger said that the State Department was in constant touch with the Syrian authorities and praised their constructive approach, while from Israel came reports of heavy United States pressure designed to stop any Israeli reaction if Syrian troops did move into Lebanon. At the same time, a seven-ship Task Force of the American Sixth Fleet moved into position near the Lebanese coast, ostensibly for possible use in evacuating foreigners from the country, though it was also noted that the force included a ship carrying 1,000 battle-ready Marines. In a series of messages to Jumblatt and Arafat, President Assad warned that the concentration of Syrian troops on the border was no bluff, and he made it plain that not only was he prepared to use his forces but that he had been given the all-clear to do so by the world community. Jumblatt admitted he had been warned to end the conflict and with his more moderate deputy, Abbas Khalaf, held lengthy meetings with Arafat and his number two, Salah Khalaf. Arafat was the one fighting for a truce, while Jumblatt kept finding excuses and reasons for continuing the battle, and picked on Franjieh's refusal to resign the Presidency, despite the clearly expressed wish of a majority of the Deputies, as his reason for not agreeing to a truce. 'The man seems nailed to the Presidential chair,' he said. Arafat and the Syrians had a plan ready, for they had anticipated this sticking point: the Lebanese Parliament would be recalled to amend the constitution so that a new President would be elected within six months of the end of the term of his predecessor. Attacked publicly by the groups in his own Leftist alliance which owed allegiance to Syria, such as the Ba'ath Party and the Nasserite organization, criticized for his intransigence by such Sunni leaders as Rashid Karami, Jumblatt eventually had to give in. He agreed to a week-long 'freeze' during which Parliament would meet, though he made it clear that this was not even a truce, merely a pause in the combat, during which each side would hold the positions it had reached and that if nothing was achieved by a Parliamentary meeting then the fighting would begin again.

It was Syrian pressure which had brought about this new attempt at a negotiated peace in Lebanon, but it was Egypt which had caused the Syrians to exert their maximum diplomatic and military leverage on Jumblatt. President Sadat was dismayed at the ready American acceptance of the Syrian initiative in Lebanon; he had expelled the Russians and realigned his country firmly with the West in the expectation that America would bail him out of his huge economic difficulties from a mixture of gratitude and a determination to maintain this newly achieved Middle East foothold. If Syria were to move away from the Soviet camp and drift towards the American sphere of influence, Egypt's advantage would be lost. Somehow, President Sadat had to reassert Egyptian leadership of the Arab world. He chose to do so by seeking to impose a Pan-Arab settlement of the Lebanese war. He called a meeting of the Arab League and through the Egyptian Secretary

General, Mahmoud Riad, let it be known that he intended to press for the establishment of an Arab peace-keeping force of which Egypt would supply the bulk of the troops needed. It was the knowledge of this proposal which lent urgency to the Syrian moves; if they could get a ceasefire and begin negotiations before the Egyptian proposal was formally considered, it could be headed off, and Egypt would once again be relegated to the side-lines in what had clearly become the major Arab crisis of the year.

The Syrian ploy worked: bowing to Syrian pressure, the Leftists ended their offensive, largely because the Palestinians, who always did most of the fighting, made it plain they would not go on. The Phalangists, for their part, needed little prompting to accept a new ceasefire: they were faring badly and desperately needed a breathing space. So the firing died down once more, and people emerged cautiously from their cellars and makeshift shelters as the bombardments stopped. 'Military action may be nearing an end,' Jumblatt said, though he promised that the political battle would go on. Appropriately enough, the new formal ceasefire was announced on 1 April, to go into effect at noon the next day, and this time it worked – worked in a Lebanese way, for scattered shooting and sniping continued, and eighty-five people were killed in the first twenty-four hours of this latest truce. Then the Left agreed to make the period of the 'freeze' ten days instead of a week, attempts to take ground by assault had ended, and the Syrians were obviously determined that this time they would impose a solution, if the Lebanese did not find one for themselves. Once again, there was a flicker of hope.

9

Syria the peacemaker ...

The most urgent necessity now was to amend the electoral law so that President Franjieh's successor could be chosen quickly, with the corollary that Franjieh himself could step down once that was done, though his term ran until mid-September. This was clearly what the Syrians wanted, as they showed by their continued pressure on Jumblatt not to renew the war, though fighting did go on in the mountains around Metn and Ain Tourah, and there were skirmishes in the cities. Syrian troops took the Masnaa border post about a mile inside Lebanese territory and also Deir al Achaya, the frontier village which marked the beginning of the Arafat Trail to the Arkoub, thus ensuring control of overland arms' supplies. At the same time more men were sent into Lebanon to bring the total P.L.A. strength in the country to eight battalions – though until then no-one would have thought the Syrian Army had as many as eight Palestinian battalions. On 10 April, eighty-nine of the total ninety-nine Parliamentary Deputies were able to get to a meeting at the spacious sandstone Villa Esseily next to the barracks in Avenue Fouad al Awal, close to the Green Line, as it was becoming known, the line dividing Beirut into Christian and Moslem Zones with the sole hazardous crossing point at the National Museum. Brigadier Ahdab's men provided what security there was for this bizarre Parliamentary gathering, though each Deputy brought his own armed escort, which gave rise to some desperate moments as Phalangist and Moslem guards faced each other at point-blank range. Somehow the men of the Beirut Army garrison managed to prevent any mayhem, even when mortars dropped nearby and each side assumed itself to be the target and its opponents the attackers. So with unusual expedition the

Deputies passed a bill amending Article 73 of the Constitution, which cleared the way for the election of a new President to be arranged immediately, rather than within a few weeks of the end of Franjieh's term.

The Deputies' sense of urgency as they passed the Bill was due not only to the physical danger all around them but also to the whole deteriorating situation: as well as the fighting in the mountains, Syria had begun a blockade of Sidon to prevent arms reaching the Palestinians – a British ship, the *Cheshire Venture*, was fired on by a gunboat – while in Beirut, sporadic exchanges of fire were liable to start the whole battle again; a Rightist mortar bombardment of the Murr Tower, held by the Mourabitoun, closed things down as shells fell far wide of their target. Still, Jumblatt was persuaded to extend the ten-day 'freeze' to which he had previously agreed, largely as a result of the new Syrian threats: in addition to seizing the 'bridgeheads' inside Lebanon, tanks had been deployed in the Bekaa Valley as President Assad warned once again that he was quite prepared to send his Army in if need be. 'We are ready to move in at any time, to face any aggressor, no matter what his religious persuasion,' Assad said in a clear indication that, if he did act, the enemy would be the Moslem Palestinians and their allies. 'Syria has complete freedom,' he added, pointedly dashing any lingering hopes that he might be inhibited by American or Israeli pressure. Israel announced that it had established 'a red line' beyond which Syrian troops would not be able to go without provoking some response; but this line seemed to be in the minds of the politicians rather than having an existence on any general's map and was never invoked; it was intended solely as a domestic palliative, for in fact Israel had received clear assurance via America that Syria would not seek to occupy border areas or to use Lebanon for any action against Israel. Syria seemed ready to do what the Israelis would have liked to do themselves, something they had failed to achieve in all the years of conflict: to subdue the Palestinians. That, at least, was how the Israelis saw it and how the Palestinians themselves were coming to view the situation, for day after day the Syrians gave new and deliberate evidence of their intentions in an effort to get what they wanted by persuasion rather than by force of arms. In the middle of

April a reconnaissance unit of two armoured cars and four jeep-loads of Syrian soldiers deliberately and ostentatiously moved out of the Syrian advance headquarters near Masnaa and headed along the road to Beirut, knowing full well from aerial surveillance that this highway was held by the Lebanese Arab Army, a force which the Syrians would have welcomed in earlier times: now the recce unit seemed intent on provoking a confrontation, perhaps to provide the excuse which might trigger a full-scale invasion. However, when soldiers holding a strong and easily defended position on the heights at Deir al Baida threatened to open fire, Lieutenant Khatib himself hurriedly arrived on the scene and ended the incident with handshakes and embraces rather than bullets and bombs.

Under the menace of direct Syrian action, Arafat went to Damascus yet again, and on his return the twenty-seventh ceasefire was proclaimed against a background of rival mortar barrages; still, the Truce Supervisory Committee was reactivated with representatives of all sides agreeing to take part and even more important, after days of procrastination, Franjieh finally signed the decree which formalized the law permitting the election of a new President, though at the same time he made it clear he had no intention of resigning before his term was up. This move gave people's spirits something of a lift, for it had long been heralded as the precursor of a political settlement; but, as usual, there were those still out to continue the war. On 19 April fifteen Christians were murdered in revenge for nine Moslems who had been abducted and slaughtered two days earlier; the next day Ahmed Jabril sent the men of his Popular Front – General Command back into the fray. Jabril, a member of the Rejection Front, held the Beirut sector covering the commercial district of the city; he had his headquarters in the Bahri Restaurant, once one of the best Arab eating places in the country. His men were a wild bunch, though they included some of the toughest in the Resistance Movement because Jabril's own reputation attracted the best fighters as well as the most politically fanatical. It was this reputation which drew members of international Left-wing organizations to the group: an American Negro 'Black Power' man was with them throughout the year; in his cups, which was often, he used to describe himself as 'a Palestinian from Haifa'. Others with Jabril's group were Spanish doctors and a pharmacist, and at various times members of other extremist foreign groups were also there. Jabril's own men often went into battle fortified by hashish; grown in Lebanon and regularly exported (it accounted for eleven per cent of the country's exports in the year before the war), 'Lebanese gold', as it was known, was little used inside the country except by foreigners until the war, when many Palestinians took to it, though it remained a rare phenomenon on the Christian side. A group of Jabril's men were once quietly smoking hash as they waited in a cellar to go out on a raid, but after one or two joints had gone round they ran out of matches, so one of them carefully balanced the new cigarette on the end of his Kalashnikov and pulled the trigger in the hope of lighting it. The bullets ricocheted round the stone cavern; miraculously no-one was hurt and the fighters could laugh weakly as they moved slowly out to battle.

As the fighting continued in the mountains and in Beirut with Zahle being shelled by the Left and constant skirmishing on the outskirts of Tripoli, the *de facto* partition of the country was made more complete as both sides began setting up their own administrative machinery, desperately needed if total chaos was to be averted, though it furthered the dismemberment of the country, as the Syrians warned. For it was clear that President Assad was rapidly losing patience with Kamal Jumblatt, who seemed intent on keeping the war going in any way he could. Jumblatt first said he would launch an offensive if there was not a quick meeting of Parliament to elect a new President; then he objected that the date set, 1 May, was too soon, and warned that the Left would not allow the selection of a man 'not acceptable to the people'. The truth was that Jumblatt was becoming isolated, as the Palestinians sought to rescue something from the increasingly adverse political situation, while the Left-wing leader remained committed to battle until the reforms he considered vital were agreed. Jumblatt knew that, if the Right managed to get back on top, there would be little prospect of any change and his own role would be diminished; he saw that the Palestinians wanted to end the affair on the best terms they could and so sought to keep them involved, for, without the Palestinians, Jumblatt could do nothing, despite his boasts of huge Druze forces. The Palestinians had taken over.

At least Jumblatt and Arafat were agreed on who they wanted as the next President: their choice was Raymond Edde, the sixty-two-year-old leader of the Centre Bloc in Parliament. Edde was of course a Maronite, as any Presidential candidate still had to be, though he was well outside the mainstream of Christian thought. Edde refused to leave his home in West Beirut close to the radio station which was a regular target for the Right-wing's mortars, and he prevented his followers, who lived mainly in the Jbail district around Byblos, from siding with the Phalangists or Chamoun's 'Tigers'. Edde had frequently served in Government and in recent years had led the Opposition in Parliament, where he was a great deal more outspoken than most Lebanese Deputies. He was rich enough to be incorruptible, brave enough not to be intimidated, and clever enough to restore the country to sanity and to push through the reforms so badly needed. He suffered only one disadvantage: the Syrians did not want him.

The candidate acceptable to Damascus was Elias Sarkis, the Governor of the Central Bank who had so narrowly lost to Franjieh six years earlier. Sarkis was a Chehabist, a follower of General Chehab, the Army Commander who took over as President when Camille Chamoun stepped down in 1958 at the end of that earlier civil war. Sarkis was a technocrat, a man who had been picked out by Chehab for his abilities, not for any political reason. He had been Director of the Presidential Bureau, one of the most powerful behind-the-scenes offices available, and had done very well there. At the Central Bank he was criticized for some of his *laissez faire* policies, but no-one ever accused him of corruption or stupidity, and in Lebanese public life this was a tremendous recommendation. The only disquieting things about Sarkis, for most people, were his lack of any political base and his negative public persona. Without any following of his own, it was thought, Sarkis would be dependent on the Army or on Syria; it was particularly noted that former members of the Deuxième Bureau, the men who had run the country during the administrations of Chehab and Helou, and who had been exiled to Syria, were now acting as intermediaries between Sarkis and the Syrian authorities.

There was also some bewilderment over Sarkis's position during the war: he had made no pronouncements, taken no sides and offered no solutions. The result was that no-one knew just what he would do if he were to be elected, and the answers he gave when questioned were evasive in the extreme. Sarkis was very clearly keeping all options open, and the result was that it was impossible to find out where he stood.

Yet, when the day came, he was easily elected. This was not for his own undoubted merits but because the Syrians wanted him, and saw to it that enough people turned up in Parliament and voted the way they wanted. Syrian helicopters and armoured cars were sent to bring in reluctant Deputies, so long as it was known they would vote as required; Syrian officers directed the P.L.A. troops outside Parliament as mortars fell nearby and the rattle of machine-gun fire echoed through the deserted streets – never can a President have been chosen against a more appropriate or a more daunting background. For a long time it looked as if the election would have to be postponed, for by 1 p.m. only sixty-four of the people's representatives had made it to the dangerous Green Line meeting place; then three more arrived together to bring the total over the two-thirds quorum needed, and eventually sixty-nine turned up. On the first ballot Sarkis got only sixty-three votes, but some hasty lobbying and a few more mortar bombs close outside ensured sixty-eight on the second ballot with only one stubborn Deputy still refusing to endorse this Syrian-imposed candidate. This was enough: Sarkis was declared duly elected and the Deputies hurried away, many of them forced to run crouched to their waiting cars as bullets whipped overhead. Sarkis himself was not spared the violence: he was staying at the Carlton Hotel in West Beirut during the period of the election – significantly, guarded by men said to be members of Saiqa, who were in reality Syrian soldiers. The hotel was attacked by a group of gunmen from one of the Rejection Front groups and it was three hours before the attackers were driven off, with the loss of four of the Saiqa defenders. Hardly the usual inaugural ceremony for a new Head of State.

The actual election did give rise to high hopes, however; it was widely anticipated, not least by Sarkis, that President Franjieh would step down and allow the new man to take over.

But Franjieh showed no sign of doing so. At his makeshift new Presidential Palace, the Town Hall at Zouk Mikail, just outside Jounieh, Franjieh continued to receive visitors, sign decrees, and carry on as if there had been no change. Soon he let it be known that he had no intention of leaving before the end of his mandate on 23 September, and at one stage he even found some obscure law which would allow him to remain for a pitiful further three days. The election of Sarkis seemed to have had no effect, in spite of all the effort put into it; perhaps the only real result was a clarification of the Syrian role, increasingly seen as being in direct support of the Right. So widespread was this feeling now that there were a series of armed clashes between Syrians and Leftist forces – the Syrians in the guise either of P.L.A. men or members of Saiqa. In Tripoli, both these organizations had to go into action when they were attacked by local Nasserite and Iraqi Ba'ath Party militias in another practical demonstration of the use of Lebanon as the cockpit of inter-Arab rivalries. In Beirut the situation was as bad as ever with lethal shelling by both sides: five hundred people, most of them civilians, were killed in one three-day period. In the mountains Christian troops launched a counterattack to stop the Leftist thrust towards Bikfaya and Faraya, and were repulsed when Fatah sent strong reinforcements to help the Jumblatt troops fighting there. Outside forces were coming into play too: Kuwait and Saudi Arabia had been making strenuous efforts to bring together Syria and Egypt, the two erstwhile allies whose continued estrangement was doing much to keep the Lebanese war going. Saudi Arabia offered low interest loans and reduced-price oil to President Assad if he would agree to a meeting with President Sadat, and, faced with the terrible drain on Syrian resources and the increasingly desperate economic plight of his country, Assad agreed to a summit meeting in Riyadh. It was, however, quickly nipped in the bud: hearing of what was planned, Colonel Gaddafi of Libya sent his Prime Minister, Major Abdel Salam Jalloud, to Damascus with offers matching and bettering those given by Saudi Arabia on condition that the Riyadh meeting was abandoned. President Assad readily agreed, as he had no wish for any *rapprochement* with Egypt until he had secured all his objectives, and such a time was still a long way off. To complicate matters still further, President Giscard d'Estaing suddenly invaded the scene with a casual offer, made during a visit to America, of 'several Regiments' of French troops for peace-keeping duties in Lebanon. Not surprisingly, the Left were instantly suspicious of this move from a nation traditionally identified with the Maronites of the country; so too were the other European Powers, who saw in the French move much more than the casual brainchild of the French President which it later turned out to have been.

While the inter-Arab and international bargaining and bickering went on, there were new moves towards establishing local administrations in the Christian and Moslem areas of Lebanon now nearly formalized into separate mini-states. The Green Line dividing Beirut was accepted as a fact of life as real as the Berlin Wall and just as dangerous. The Museum crossing place was a daily hazard for those whose occupations forced them to go back and forth: mainly journalists trying to cover both sides of the war, since Christians or Moslems re-settling in their own areas had to make the journey only once. Edouard Saab, the editor of the French language Beirut newspaper *L'Orient* and correspondent of *Le Monde*, was killed while driving his car there, the twelfth journalist to die in the war. By tacit agreement, there was a brief truce each morning as parcels of *An Nahar* were passed from West to East Beirut and *Al Amal*, the Phalangist paper, from East to West; but there were no similar arrangements for the men who had to write for these newspapers. On each side of the line, efforts were being made to impose some sort of normal life in spite of all the daily batterings by weapons of all kinds. In the Moslem sectors, the Mourabitoun and el Fatah sent out regular security patrols in place of the police, who had long since disappeared; on the Christian side, the Phalangists did the same and soon the establishment of the Moslem Popular Security Forces was matched by the Service Kataeb de Sécurité of the Right (the Kataeb was the Arabic name for the Phalangist Party). Garbage-collectors were found to clear some of the huge piles of stinking rubbish from the streets – until now, local people had been burning it each evening, so that the streets were constantly filled with the acrid fumes of these rubbish fires – which seemed to make no difference to the number of flies about or to the explosion of the cat population, which thrived on the tips, and fortunately matched and checked the rise in the number of rats. On both sides, electricians, telephone engineers and water-board men somehow kept a basic service going for most of the time, though eventually water was available only at certain mains in the streets and electricity was completely cut off, to be restored for only a few hours each day.

The fighting was going on steadily regardless of all the announcements of fresh ceasefires and appeals from various leaders; and there was a new phenomenon, too: battles between groups supposedly on the same side. On the Left, this was understandable as the realization filtered down to the lowest ranks that Syria, and therefore Saiqa and the P.L.A. were no longer allies. The result was frequent clashes between these Syrian-dominated organizations and the men of the hard-line groups, the P.F.L.P. and others in the Rejection Front. Often the cause would be a Saiqa or P.L.A. attempt to stop the extremists collecting ammunition or supplies; at least twenty P.F.L.P. men were killed in a shoot-out near the airport when Saiqa held up a consignment of ammunition they tried to collect there. On the Right, things were more complicated: Raymond Edde and his supporters in the National Bloc in Byblos were the targets, largely because they were considered traitors to the Maronite cause. The Christians now regarded Syria as their ally, and Edde's opposition to any armed intervention from Damascus was seen as a sign of his support of the Left, in the same way that his continued residence in West Beirut and his outspoken condemnation of excesses by either side were believed to be tactics designed to ingratiate him with the Palestinians. Edde had always been the most down-to-earth of all Lebanese politicians, a man who pursued a lonely course and had probably missed office as a consequence; this time, he almost lost his life because of his attitude. A number of Phalangists jeered and heckled in deliberate provocation while Edde was holding a meeting in Byblos – and in Lebanon opponents never made their presence known at the meetings of another political party for fear of violence. These three hecklers were determined to cause trouble and got it. First, they were beaten up, then two of them were shot, and soon large numbers of their friends were on the scene seeking vengeance. A fire-fight started and Edde had to take shelter in a house nearby, where a rocket narrowly missed him. Two Phalangists, eleven of Edde's men, and seventeen unfortunate local residents were killed before Edde himself managed to escape. Then, next day, his motorcade was halted at what appeared to be a regular road-block at Nahr Ibrahim, between Jounieh and Beirut. As the cars stopped, Phalangists hidden nearby opened fire and Edde was wounded in the foot. At almost the same time, Fatah and Saiqa were fighting it out near Sidon, as the last traces of order in the country seemed to be crumbling and total anarchy taking over. The attack on Edde was particularly disturbing, because individual politicians had never before been singled out and, though each of them always moved about with bodyguards, it would not have been possible to ensure total security. The situation was made worse a few days later when gunmen knocked on the door of the house occupied by Mrs Lilian al Atrash, Kamal Jumblatt's sister. With her two daughters she was living near the Green Line, in Christian territory. She was shot dead and her two daughters wounded in what looked like a deliberate attempt to intimidate Moslem residents of the area, as well as to hurt the leader of the Left.

While these individual acts of terror were going on so, too, was the general fighting; fifteen people were killed when a shell hit a queue waiting for a cinema (cinemas were still open for afternoon shows only). Ten children died when another shell landed on a kindergarten in Tal Zaatar; dozens of others were killed by the daily random mortaring of Achrafiyah. The airport, which was still operating, was in trouble in two ways; Christian gunners in the hills near Baabda had it in their sights and opened fire in protest if they thought arms shipments were coming in; and the Syrians in the guise of Saiqa men controlled the approaches to the airport from Beirut. Only Middle East Airlines was trying to maintain a service with all its planes overnighting in other places and its operational headquarters moved to Athens, while the staff needed at the airport lived a precarious existence there and were never able to go to their homes.

In the last days of May, events took on a new momentum. Most important of all, Syria renewed the United Nations mandate to police the armistice line with Israel with no public bargaining and no attempt at the usual cliff-hanging diplomacy. In the past, the six monthly renewals of the U.N. force's status in the Golan had been opportunities for the Syrians to extract some new concessions – it was on one of these occasions that Syria managed to persuade the Security Council to hear the representative of the Palestine Liberation Organization in a Middle East debate. This time, there was no argument. Clearly the Syrians had other things to think about; in fact they had already been given the private assurances they sought, so that there was no need for public brinkmanship. Pierre Gemayel gave a hint of what was afoot: last January, he said, the Americans had stopped the Syrians sending their troops into Lebanon as President Assad had wanted to do. And this Phalangist leader, who had earlier said he and his men would fight to the last drop of blood to halt a Syrian invasion, criticized the Americans for not allowing the Syrians to do what they wanted.

All that was needed for the Syrians to move was an excuse and this was provided by Major Ahmed Maamari, the fire-eating Commander of the Lebanese Arab Army units in the north of the country who had earlier threatened to 'raze' Zghorta. Now the Major was besieging two Christian villages in the Akkar: Qubeiyat and Andqit. The people of these two substantial settlements were reported to have appealed to President Assad for help, though how they could have done so was not explained. Certainly their spokesmen made it sound as if they were in a desperate plight with the defence provided only by a small contingent of Christian soldiers stationed there under the command of a Captain, while the attackers had far greater forces and had also brought up field artillery with which they were said to be shelling the towns. At least two hundred homes were reported to have been flattened in a steady bombardment and, according to carefully repeated broadcasts from the Phalangist radio, the townspeople were sure they would be massacred if help was not forthcoming.

Jumblatt and Arafat both asked Major Maamari to pull back; they saw the emerging pattern and hoped to avoid giving

Syria the final excuse for moving in. They were too late, for Major Maamari had been secretly to Damascus the previous week and had been given his orders, which were entirely opposed to those sent by Jumblatt and Arafat. The Major took no notice of the requests, the almost pleading demands for an end to his attacks: 'I intend to destroy these towns if Franjieh does not give up the Presidency,' he said.

As affairs moved to a new climax, more terrible weapons than any employed before made their appearance in the streets of Beirut. Palestinian gunners set up Soviet-made Grad missiles, tubes of high explosive two yards long which could cause devastation over a huge area when they landed. As they were fired, the noise caused almost as much panic as the missiles did when they landed, for they were highly inaccurate and few hit any chosen targets. The Right were prepared for this escalation and had their answer ready: French-built SS11 missiles were in place and were used to reply to the bombardment, again with little more success than that enjoyed by the artillerymen with the Grads. There was an increase in political tension, too: Zuheir Mohsen, the Saiqa Commander, made a speech attacking Jumblatt by name and talking of the 'Rightist' element in the Palestinian leadership – a clear reference to Arafat. The stage was being set for the full-scale Syrian invasion which had been threatened for so long. The Palestinians were making their own final preparations for it, too, by withdrawing units from the confrontation lines with the Phalangists and sending them to defend the eastern approaches to Beirut and to positions around Saiqa camps and strongholds. Arafat had no illusions about where the real loyalties of the Saiqa men lay and was quickly proved right.

On 1 June the Syrians moved. In the North, two thousand regular Syrian troops with sixty tanks went to the rescue of Qubeiyat and Andqit, while four thousand men with two hundred tanks rolled across the main road at Masnaa to relieve the pressure on Zahle. The final phase of the Lebanese war had begun and though the fighting continued for another six months, it was the beginning of the end.

10

... peace with tanks

The initial Syrian thrusts met no opposition. The Palestinians and Leftists faded away in front of the Syrian armour, making no attempt to stand and fight; many did not even bother to retreat, but merely stayed quietly outside the positions from which they had been firing at the Phalangists a few minutes before and waved cordially to the Syrian tank crews as they rolled past. The Syrian detachments which followed were specially picked and highly political; these were not the usual tough infantry groups which follow a tank invasion, but units of the Special Forces capable of deciding on the spot what to do with the Palestinians and Lebanese who had been overrun. The attackers' first objective seemed to be not military but diplomatic: they wanted a 'legal' pretext for the invasion and easily found it in Qubeiyat at a hastily arranged conference that seemed to confirm all the suspicions about Major Maamari which had been voiced. The Major, with his forces, waited for the Syrian Army to reach him, then readily agreed to a meeting with Captain George Maakia, who was in charge of the defence of both Qubeiyat and Andqit; the two officers quickly reached an agreement on the separation of their troops, under the watchful eyes of Syrian 'observers', who went on to a meeting with the notables of the town. At this conference, according to Lebanese officials, the Syrians produced an already written document for them to sign: this set out the thanks of the townspeople for their rescue by the Syrians, affirmed that they had been in danger of being massacred, then went on to outline a highly political series of objectives which these simple people of the Akkar were supposed to have put to the Syrian officers. With Major Maamari and Captain Maakia sipping coffee together and the Mukhtar and other officials obligingly signing when and where they were told, the whole affair was a very obvious charade. A similar event took place at Zahle, but at least it was done with rather more finesse and privacy: Joseph Skaf, the Deputy for the area, in turn appealed to President Assad to help, and to lift the siege of Zahle imposed by the Palestinians. The Syrian leader said he would be prepared to do so, but demanded a request in writing, and it was Syrian envoys who obligingly helped Skaf to formulate his plea in a way which would ensure Syrian intervention.

So the Syrian columns seized their first objectives in the Bekaa Valley and linked up with the P.L.A. and Saiqa units there; the Phalangists cheerfully abandoned their positions, then announced they had been forced to move out. Soon the Bekaa was as peaceful as it had ever been with the dozens of restaurants for which Zahle was famous doing roaring business and happily accepting Syrian lira, not a gun in sight, and the peasants beginning the task of repairing the damage to their homes and to the vital irrigation systems caused by more than a year of war. The Syrians, meanwhile, took over buildings for their headquarters, sited their artillery and tanks, and set up road-blocks to control all traffic. It was a very low-key invasion in this first phase and provoked none of the anguished cries which might have been expected from other Arab countries, and no adverse response at all from the rest of the world: Dr Kissinger again gave Damascus his blessing, and as Alexei Kosygin, the Russian Prime Minister, had been in Damascus the day the Syrian troops moved, there was little the Soviets could say about it; Israel, for its part, kept unusually quiet.

By 3 June, the Syrian regulars had done no more than fan out into the Bekaa Valley and take over control of the vital Chtaura crossroads from the P.L.A. They pushed along the highway until they came within sight of the Palestinians' main defence line on the ridge at Deir al Baida, just above Chtaura. There the Palestinians had cut trenches across the road to stop the tanks, dug anti-tank weapons into well-concealed emplacements on the surrounding hills, and deployed their best troops. 'We stay here,' said a young Palestinian officer. 'They will have to kill us all before they get through here.' It was something of an anti-climax when the Syrians stopped some four hundred yards short of this dramatic defence line, casually pulled their tanks off the road, and nonchalantly set up a flimsy barricade of wire to control the few pedestrians who ventured through. The Syrian troops seemed a great deal more interested in the two or three main shops of Chtaura and the marvellous cherries from the orchards nearby than in the Palestinian defenders. The Syrian officers, too, were more intent on making friends with the local people than rooting out the opposition; they kissed children and shook hands with men as if they were on an election campaign rather than a military expedition.

This phase could not last and the true situation became apparent as a second Syrian armoured column wound its way over the hills towards Sidon. Once within sight of this port city, the Syrians put in a deadly softening-up barrage and drew no fire at all in return. Assuming that the Palestinians had pulled out, the invaders sent a strong advance party down into the town with tanks, armoured personnel carriers and armoured cars. The convoy drove slowly down the hill from Ein el Deleb and into the first narrow streets of Sidon; as soon as all the vehicles were inside the confines of the city and over-looked by houses on either side, the waiting Palestinians opened up a murderous fire. Carefully sited anti-tank guns went into action with devastating effect; rocket-propelled grenades thundered out, recoilless rifles boomed and heavy machine-guns sought the narrow gaps in the armour. Two tanks were knocked out right away, four more were captured with their crews, and the rest scrambled hastily out of this well-prepared trap. The Syrians put in a new bombardment, then tried again. This time it was an even more desperate affair: attacking in two thrusts, the Syrians got right to the centre of the town. Anticipating this, the Palestinians had somehow man-handled a 25-pound field gun up into a building and, when the Syrian lead tank paused uncertainly at the round-about in the city centre, not sure which way to turn, the artillerymen wound the gun down to maximum depression and fired a shot head-on into the tank at a range of about one hundred yards. The tank exploded in a tangle of steel as its load of ammunition went up; the turret was blown twenty yards into the air and landed on the roof of an adjacent house, where it stayed for months, a symbol of the defence of Sidon.

After this, the Syrians withdrew; they pulled back in good order and regrouped just above the town, waiting for new instructions, but none came. Just wait, they were told; for things had gone badly wrong and the High Command in Damascus, as well as the task force commanders on the spot, had to deal with a wholly unexpected situation.

The trouble was that in the week between the original incursion and the advance on Sidon, which was matched by an attack on the town of Bhamdoun, twelve miles from Beirut, the Palestinians had diminished the support on which the Syrians were relying: they had fought and beaten the Saiqa forces in the country, and prevented the P.L.A. units loyal to Syria from moving to the assistance of their masters. As soon as the Syrian invasion began, Arafat had formed a Central Military Command of the Resistance Movement, which included every organization except Saiqa; the moderate Fatah and the extremist Rejection Front organizations were united as never before in the face of the Syrian threat. Foolishly, the Syrians gave the Palestinians time to act. If the tanks had rolled straight into Beirut and Sidon in the first forty-eight hours, nothing could have stopped a total Syrian take-over of Lebanon; but that did not happen, for President Assad had to pursue a cautious policy: he had to gauge Arab and international opinion at every stage, and he was also inhibited by his need to avoid casualties as far as possible, and to keep things quiet inside his own country. It was no easy task for him suddenly to present the Palestinians as the enemy after years of propaganda in which they had been lauded as freedom fighters and comrades; nor was it easy to explain to the Syrian soldiers why they were suddenly being rotated between the Iraqi border and Lebanon, with the Golan Plateau, until now their main centre of activity, as a very subsidiary theatre of operations. Heavy casualties could not have been concealed from the populace and could well have given rise to unrest inside a country more prone to coups than most. Some five hundred junior officers had been arrested or transferred and the rest sufficiently indoctrinated not to cause trouble; but the situation in his army and his country was a factor which President Assad had to consider at all times. His plan, therefore, had been to let the P.L.A. and Saiqa do most of the work for him, so that the Syrian troops sent pouring into Lebanon would merely take over as 'a peace-keeping force', as the Syrians liked to call it, separating the combatants in the country and using their muscle only when it was needed to prevent more violence. This plan might well have worked if the Syrian surrogates had done their job properly; but they could not. Saiqa forces held the airport in Beirut and the approaches to it, and were reinforced by air from Syria, while another group was in command of the main coastal highway at Khalde. In Sidon, the Syrian commando organization held positions in the low hills above the town and also had its cells in the city itself. All seemed to have been well prepared, until on 7 June Arafat sent his men into action: first the isolated pockets of Saiqa men in the refugee camps around Beirut and Sidon were cleared out in a classic surprise operation; then the Resistance men moved on the main forces. This was a different matter, for the Saiqa troops at the airport, at Khalde and above Sidon were in the main regular Syrian soldiers in commando uniform, and they had been supplied with light artillery. The Fatah men and their allies could make little headway, and were taking a lot of punishment, particularly when the Saiqa guns opened up on Chatila and Sabra camps before the force occupying the airport stormed down the long road into the town in an effort to take up their previously assigned positions for the link-up with the Syrian invasion column. This was the crucial moment, for if the Saiqa troops had succeeded in their objectives there is little doubt that Syria would have occupied Beirut and Sidon, and the war would have been over entirely on Syrian terms. As it was, the Resistance men held the line: in Beirut, the attack was halted in bitter fighting around the Kuwait Embassy crossroads and the inappropriately named Camille Chamoun Stadium. Battling it out in the most desperate form of street warfare, so close that grenades and pistols were sometimes used, the Fatah men halted the Saiqa thrust and pushed their one-time colleagues back to the airport. At Khalde a similar break-out was blunted, and in the South the Saiqa men were scattered and disorganized by lethal artillery fire on their exposed hillside positions.

The result of all this was to nullify the Syrian plan, as the aim of the attackers was to invest Sidon, then link up in Beirut in a two-pronged move. The column sent over the hills through Jezzin to Sidon was the more powerful and larger of the two attacking forces, for once at Sidon it was supposed to split up with one group holding the city and sending forces south to Tyre when appropriate, another moving quickly north to take the Zahrani refinery and prevent it from being sabotaged, and a third to press on to Beirut to link up with the column attacking directly down the main Damascus–Beirut highway which had been carefully held back so that it should not arrive in Beirut too soon. All these moves depended on the help of Saiqa men, not only to contain most of the opposition before the regular forces arrived, so that the Syrians could be presented as liberators, but also to act as guides. And it was because none of the designated guides could carry out their functions that the Syrian attack on Sidon failed, and the other moves were halted in consequence. Lists of names of Syrian–Palestinian Saiqa men were found on captured Syrian officers with meeting places marked on their maps and their objectives named. When the guides did not turn up, the Syrians were lost; if that lead tank in the main street of Sidon had known which way to turn, it might have avoided that point-blank shell, and, if the Palestinians had not had such huge and obvious success, perhaps their resistance would have crumbled. There were dozens of imponderables, but the fact remained that after their reverse in Sidon the Syrians stopped. On the Damascus road into Beirut there was no real need for them to have done so, for they had quickly reduced the Palestinians' carefully prepared positions at Deir al Baida. Lebanese jets from the captured Rayek base had done the trick; when they seized this military airfield, the biggest in the country, the Syrians had gathered the officers together and given them a straight choice: would they like to throw in their lot with the Syrians, whose only aim was to save Lebanon from anarchy and the domination of the foreign Palestinians who were the real cause of all the troubles in the country, or would they prefer to go to a prison camp in Syria until the affair was ended? It was not difficult for the Air Force officers, most of them Christians, to decide what to do. Lieutenant-Colonel Fahim Haj was made the base commander, all those willing to work with the Syrians were enrolled in a force called The Vanguards of the

Lebanese Army, which was intended to be the nucleus of a new Lebanese military force on which to build in the future, and Major Mohammed Mattar was put in command of the three planes which were found capable of flying. Major Mattar and his co-pilots gave swift proof of their loyalty to their new masters: they flew several sorties against the Palestinians on the ridge above Chtaura, then screamed down into Beirut to hit Palestinian concentrations there. After the air-strike, the Syrian tanks moved forward and their only check came as infantrymen quickly filled in the anti-tank ditches the Palestinians had dug. These tough defenders had pulled out without making any attempt to halt the advance.

It was among the orchards of Bhamdoun, twelve miles from Beirut, that they did stand and fight. They were not too effective and, if the Syrians had been determined, they could easily have pushed through; but by this time news of the trouble at Sidon had reached the Syrian commanders and a halt was ordered. Though it did not look like it at the time, the Syrian invasion had been stopped and the positions reached hardly altered for months to come. The Palestinians did not realize this: they were talking of a last desperate stand in the Lebanese capital itself and, whether or not that would actually have taken place, they were certainly preparing for it. Families were unceremoniously ejected from their homes on the outskirts of the city as building after building was taken over to be turned into a blockhouse. Strong-points were picked out, carefully concealed guns put in position, trenches dug and shelters chosen in a frenzy of activity. And all the time the shelling went on, either from the Saiqa men at the airport and Khalde, or from the Phalangists in East Beirut who now decided to take a hand. A stray shell from the Palestinians had damaged the power station at Zouk Mikail, so the city had no power and, because of this, no water; all communications were cut, food was desperately short and petrol unobtainable. Colonel Abdel Sha'ar, a P.L.A. officer who had been put in command of all the Palestinian militias in Beirut, was killed by a chance round, which added to the general confusion and the growing fears that this was the Palestinians' final defeat, the beginning of a Black June which was to make what had happened in Jordan in 1970 appear a mere curtain-raiser to the final annihilation.

The airport was closed, so that now Beirut was cut off from the world, while Sidon was surrounded by Syrian forces; nothing could be hoped for that way. Yet the Palestinians fought on with a tenacity bred of despair, and a sort of life was maintained. Emergency generators were found and minimal communications restored, though their main use seemed to be to allow a few to watch the programmes still being put out on the television network: a two-hour festival of Laurel and Hardy with Arabic sub-titles.

The situation, however, was not as desperate as the Palestinians feared. By adopting the plan he did, President Assad had given time for those opposed to him to mobilize, and already the Arab world was in ferment. Abdel Salam Jalloud, the Libyan Prime Minister, flew in to Damascus to be joined by Algerian Foreign Minister Abdel Mahmoud; Iraq ordered a general mobilization as Sidam Hussein made a bitter radio denunciation of the Syrian invasion; Abdel Halim Khaddam flew to Libya to meet Arafat, while in Cairo Egypt hastily convened an emergency meeting of the Arab League; and Russia denounced 'foreign intervention' in Lebanon and sent a seven-ship task force to the area, to be matched by an equal American presence. Just as the Palestinians were preparing for a final stand, the dissensions in the Arab world were making it unnecessary, though in fact it was only Iraq and Libya which were genuinely opposed to the Syrian moves. Egypt, for all its rhetoric, secretly welcomed Syrian efforts to cut the Palestinians down to size, while objecting bitterly to the increased power and influence such a move would give to President Assad. Kuwait, Saudi Arabia and the other paymasters of the Gulf were just as eager to see the extremist Palestinians curbed or even to see an end to the whole problem, so that they could get on with the far more pressing task of developing their own region. Algeria was preoccupied with its problems with Morocco and Mauritania in the Sahara; Tunisia under the ageing Boumedienne had ceased to play a pan-Arab role; and the rest of the world neither understood nor cared about what was going on in Lebanon.

In the face of the uproar he had caused, President Assad for once seemed to lose his grip; he announced that his forces were to be joined by 'symbolic units' of Libyan and Algerian troops who would help in restoring peace, a transparent move designed to head off the expected decision of the Arab League Foreign Ministers who were meeting in Cairo. It did no good for the Ministers, as anticipated, took the first steps towards 'Arabizing' the Lebanese situation by calling for the withdrawal of Syrian troops and their replacement by an Arab peace-keeping force. Assad had to accept this with as much grace as he could, for there was nothing else to be done: he had missed his chance to settle the Lebanese situation swiftly and on his own terms, because he could not risk the possible repercussions inside Syria and in the Army – it was this which worried him far more than any Arab or international reaction. By the middle of June the immediate crisis was over for the Palestinians, though it was continuing for the Syrians. Already President Assad had his Third Armoured Division supported by the Seventh Division in Lebanon, and now he had to send three brigades to the Iraqi border to counter the threat posed by the troops dispatched from Baghdad. With the cost of the Lebanese operations alone running at £1,000,000 a day, the well-publicized defection of an Air Force pilot with his plane to Iraq, the first of a series of bomb explosions in Damascus, and simmering unrest which caused the mobilization of all Rifaat Assad's Special Forces, Syria was in no condition to dictate to Lebanon as it had done in the past. A period of rest and recuperation was needed, and some hard thinking; Assad even had to cut short a long-heralded European tour.

Abdel Salam Jalloud was now the most important single figure on the scene. His aim was two-fold: he wanted to keep Syria out of the clutches of the Conservative Arab régimes headed by Saudi Arabia, and he had to save the Palestinians from total subjugation. He worked as hard as any man could, constantly shuttling between Damascus and Beirut, spending long hours in meetings, and frequently displaying great personal bravery in his efforts to meet people of all sides in the various parts of the country – he was holed up at the airport for twenty hours on one occasion, as bitter fighting made it impossible for him to move into Beirut. Jalloud did all he could and occasionally appeared to have some success, not least because he often berated Palestinian leaders as strongly as he attacked the Rightists. But, at the end of the day, he achieved nothing; as one veteran said, 'He was a boy among men. He just had no idea of the intricacies of what was going on, of all the double dealing.'

And there were certainly some very odd things happening, not least the formation of the Arab peace-keeping force which was supposed to be dispatched to Lebanon as soon as possible to separate the combatants. Three countries immediately volunteered to send troops: Sudan, Saudi Arabia and Libya. It was decided, by some of the political manoeuvring for which the Arab League was famous, that an Egyptian general should be in command, though the first troops actually to arrive were the Libyans, who of course had to go in via Damascus. On their first appearance there they looked a very make-shift lot with hastily painted white bands on their helmets and only the most basic weapons, but by the time they moved into Lebanon they appeared a great deal more warlike with rocket-launchers, machine-guns and anti-tank weapons. For a peace-keeping group, they seemed fairly bellicose, lending weight to later Right-wing charges that the Libyans in fact fought on the side of the Palestinians around Jezzin. There was more confusion, too, when a contingent of troops flew in to Beirut Airport: the radio controlled by the Left reported that they were Sudanese, and there was great rejoicing at the thought of Arab peace-keepers replacing the Saiqa and Syrian forces which had occupied the airport and thus regularly shelled Palestinian positions in the town; not until a day or so later was it discovered that the reinforcements were in fact regular Syrian troops who had exchanged their regulation khaki helmets for the green berets and white helmets of the peace force.

As Syria lifted the siege of Beirut to allow in food and petrol, and at the same time began withdrawing its forces from the positions closest to Sidon, there was a new example of the lawlessness and anarchy in the Palestinian-controlled sectors of Beirut which did no good at all for the Palestinian cause: the American Ambassador, Francis Meloy, was murdered by gunmen as he drove from his embassy for a meeting in the Christian-controlled sector with Elias Sarkis. The Economic Counsellor at the embassy, Robert Waring, and their chauffeur, Zuheir Moghrabi, were also killed at the same time. The three were just a tiny fraction of those killed every day, but their deaths served to focus attention on the state of turmoil in the country, and to bring home to outside governments the dangers their diplomats had to face. In point of fact, bungling and inefficiency on the part of the American Embassy contributed to the tragedy, as no effort had been made to arrange a safe-conduct for the Ambassador through the most hazardous section he had to traverse, his bodyguards were dropped off at least a block earlier than they should have been and, when a member of Sarkis's staff telephoned to enquire where Meloy was, instead of raising the alarm, embassy officials calmly suggested he might have made another call first. The direct result of Meloy's death was an American decision to evacuate all United States citizens from Lebanon, and preparations were made to mount an air-rescue operation. The Akrotiri base in Cyprus was put on full alert with American and British C130s standing by there to take refugees out once they had reached Cyprus, and U.S. helicopters, protected by gunships, were ready to go in. At the last moment, wiser counsels prevailed and the air operation was abandoned, because of the danger that it would provoke resistance; instead, it was decided to negotiate for a seaborne evacuation and, because America was still officially unable to recognize the P.L.O., British diplomats acted as intermediaries to arrange for the seaborne operation to be allowed. A further precaution was taken, too: American officials held quiet talks with the Russians to ensure that there would be no repercussions, for Russia still had its task force off the Lebanese coast. Eventually, an agreement was reached which would permit the Americans to land a battalion of marines to establish and hold a safe bridgehead during the evacuation if there was any resistance when the landing craft which was to ferry people out first appeared. The Russians undertook not to interfere provided the Americans held only the immediate area of the evacuation point for a limited time and used their air power only to protect that bridgehead, not to enlarge the conflict. In the event, there was no need for any show of strength at all: a landing craft, with ostentatiously unarmed sailors on show, and half a dozen carefully chosen and well concealed marksmen ready to give protective fire if necessary, coasted in to the jetty at the Bain Militaire to take 263 people to the mother ship, the *Spiegel Grove*, which was lying off shore. The carrier *America* was only a hundred miles away with its plane crews waiting in their cockpits as the operation went on; an assault force of 150 marines was also aboard the vessel, in full battle kit and ready to go in to Beirut by helicopter if there was any hitch.

The murder of the Ambassador and the American evacuation, for all their dramatic impact in the West, were mere sideshows in the continuing drama of the war; much more important was the final arrival of the Arab League peace-keeping force, which was greeted with celebratory gunfire by the Palestinians and a glum silence by the Christians, who would have liked to see President Giscard's offer of French troops taken up to balance the Arab forces, which they rightly thought likely to be hostile. Jalloud, after weeks of work, jubilantly proclaimed that he had 'created a miracle', as he announced yet another ceasefire; this one did have some basis of give and take, and involved the Syrians and the Palestinians rather than the Christians. The Palestinians agreed to hand over the Saiqa, P.L.A. and Syrian soldiers they had captured (including the former P.L.A. commander, Brigadier Misbah Budeiry) in return for a Syrian withdrawal from Bhamdoun to Sofar and from Sidon to Jezzin, plus an evacuation of the airport in Beirut.

In spite of the siege of Beirut being lifted, and the Syrian withdrawal from Tripoli in the South, the war was not over: the Phalangists stepped up their attacks on Jisr al Pasha and Tal Zaatar, and a new suburban front was opened at Nabaa, another Moslem enclave in the Christian eastern sector inhabited mainly by poor Shia from Baalbeck and the South. Mortar exchanges went on, though the shelling of the airport ended and planes were able to get in and out again after a seventeen-day break; four days later came the final shut-down of this last real link with the outside world as an M.E.A. Boeing 707 was hit by a shell and the captain killed, and gunfire again made it impossible for the runways to be used. The water and electricity which had been partially restored were off again; the hesitant attempts to set up local administrations on both sides seemed to be making little headway and were having only small practical effect, so that the situation again appeared to be back to square one. At least the Syrians were carrying out their promise to withdraw from various areas and the Arab League had succeeded in getting together some reinforcements for the peace force: Saudi Arabian and Sudanese troops flew in, and, after waiting ineffectually at the airport while their commanders tried to negotiate their way out, they were eventually allowed to move into Beirut itself. But it was only the Palestinians who permitted the peace-keepers to move, and then only under sufferance; the Right would not agree to any deployment on their side of the line and, when the white-helmeted troops did try to move over to the Christian side of the Green Line at the Museum, Chamoun's men opened up with machine-guns and mortars, and forced them back.

The pressure was being maintained on the Palestinians in the camps in the East, too. Jisr al Pasha, Tal Zaatar and Nabaa were all under siege, with the N.L.P. militia and Right-wing army units pressing hardest on Tal Zaatar, the biggest of them all. This camp was entirely surrounded and cut off from all supplies, as relief columns had been driven back time after time. A hundred or so of the best Fatah men available had infiltrated in twos and threes from the mountains above the camp under cover of darkness, carrying packs of the most desperately-needed items on their backs and their rifles in their hands; it was a hazardous route and soon that too became impossible as Chamoun's men tightened the cordon. The first enclave to fall was Jisr al Pasha, overrun at the end of June; the Palestinians claimed the people in the camp had been massacred, while the Right said that all the armed men there had been killed or captured. In the welter of events no-one seemed to care; killings were an everyday occurrence, so that a few more or less made little difference. Survival was the first priority, and Lebanese and Palestinians alike, whatever their religious or political affiliations, had become numbed to horrors; their only aim was to keep themselves alive and with food, water and electricity all rare commodities, shell-fire and mortar bombardments occurring everyday, this took up everybody's time.

In a desperate plan to take the pressure off their camps in East Beirut, the Palestinians tried the tactics which had so signally failed them before when they attempted to save Karantina and Maslakh by attacking Damour. Now they opened a new front in the North, around Chekka; and with no more effect than they had achieved in Damour. After days of heavy fighting, the Palestinians were thrown out, first from Amyoun, then from Chekka itself; meanwhile the Syrians were spreading devastation as they pulled back from the South. First they shelled the Zahrani oil refinery, setting tanks and installations ablaze, then they turned their attention to Sidon, apparently with no military objectives in mind, but merely to put down a valedictory barrage on the place where they had taken more casualties than anywhere else. While Lebanon was being eaten away, the diplomats of the Arab League states kept up their wrangling, succeeding in nothing more than issuing new appeals and instructions which no-one expected to be obeyed. Mahmoud Riad, the Secretary-General, visited Beirut briefly; his presence did no more good than that of any of the other mediators who had tried their hands. The Russians evacuated Eastern Bloc personnel from the country, Israel seized an ammunition ship on its way from Alexandria to Sidon, and America arranged another evacuation of its nationals. Again, all went well; but this time the Palestinians were very obviously the organizers of the affair and they stopped an Iraqi, an Egyptian and a Palestinian girl from going on the landing craft, though all had the qualifications to do so. One who did go, without any protest at this Palestinian control over an American operation, was the new U.S. Ambassador, Talcot Seelye. As one American Embassy man put it: 'We offered people a ride in a boat, not diplomatic protection.' So, when it was all over, President Ford felt able to send a message of thanks to the P.L.O., which America had so steadfastly refused to recognize. The United States, like Russia and the Europeans, wanted no involvement in Lebanon and was quite happy to act through its unlikely deputy, Syria.

11

The country divides

With the exodus of foreigners from Lebanon, the division of
the country which had taken place was even more apparent,
and the fact that there had always been two nations was now
physically noticeable. The Palestinians and Moslems of West
Beirut were in general darker-skinned, shorter and thinner
than the people living in the Christian East of the city. There,
the girls were better dressed, had better figures and used make-
up with far more sophistication, while the men all seemed to
be bigger and healthier. The life styles were very different, too:
in the Moslem areas, ninety per cent of the shops were closed,
either because they had been looted or because their owners
had fled – it could now be seen that the Christians had the over-
whelming share of business in the city. So everything on sale
was carted around on barrows or set out each morning on the
pavements of the streets considered the safest, to be whisked
away by car before darkness fell. In most places, the huge piles
of rubbish which had accumulated over the months were still
there, for the rudimentary municipal services set up were not
good enough to deal with all the problems, and people still
had to go out each evening with a few drops of valuable paraffin to set the tips ablaze in an effort to prevent the spread of
disease; as it was, cases of cholera had been reported and dysentery was becoming endemic. The Popular Security Forces
had been established with their headquarters near another
thoroughly looted department store in Rue Verdun, but they
were not over-effective; to avoid this new body being taken
over by any one faction, it was run by a triumvirate represent-
ing the Mourabitoun, the P.L.O. and the Rejection Front. The
result was the kind of inefficiency which always stems from
rule by committee, so that robbery, anarchy and general law-

lessness continued. It was generally better to telephone the command post of whichever faction was in control of an area where an incident occurred rather than to seek the help of the new police force, though the usual reaction was for people to take the law into their own hands. A fairly typical case came when two friends, both carrying Kalashnikovs over their shoulders, met on a pavement. They embraced warmly, slapping each other on the back and hugging in the usual exuberant Arab manner, and as they did so, one of the guns went off, sending a bullet whistling past a balcony where a man was sipping coffee. Without a word this third actor in the petty drama went inside, returned with a pistol, and taking careful aim shot one of the men in the street below. Dozens of people saw the incident, but none considered it extraordinary or a cause for action. Normal behavioural patterns had been superseded long before.

In East Beirut, things were far more civilized and normal: pavement cafés were open except during the days of the most concentrated bombardments and the majority of shops were operating, because there too it was the Christians who were the owners. Life in the Right-controlled quarters was far better organized with the new police, the S.K.S., in smart grey uniforms and odd little helmets, which at least made them readily identifiable – the Popular Security Forces had no uniforms and were hard to distinguish from the general run of armed men about the streets. Traffic was far heavier in the eastern sector, too, as the Right had an effective import system and petrol was regularly brought in, while the Palestinians managed only a very sporadic service. But it was at Jounieh, which had become the capital of Christian Lebanon, that the contrasts were most marked: there, the tiny harbour was crowded with ships, while across the bay the Tabarja Beach cove was the place where the arms shipments were unloaded. The once-exclusive yacht marina on the Kaslik side of Jounieh was taken over by the dozens of small boats which made the journey between Cyprus and Lebanon each day; a former German gunboat which could do the trip in four hours, though it usually took seven, was the most popular, though with cunning appeal to the innate snobbery of the Lebanese Christians a ferry billed as 'Anthony Quinn's yacht' won a great deal of the business. The regular immigration service was working properly, with travellers having their passports stamped in and out, and having to buy visas on entry. There was also a special additional impost for the Phalangist Party, though a firm refusal to pay brought no retaliation.

The most glaring example of all of the contrast between the Christian areas and the Moslem was probably at the Lagon Club in Jounieh. There, the rich and idle congregated throughout the summer, or the idle sons and daughters of the rich. In days gone by these were the people who had graced the pool-side at St Georges Hotel or attended the beach parties at Khalde – 'le tout Beirut' as breathless gossip columnists liked to call them. The scene was as it had always been with French preferred to Arabic, ostentatious dressing-up more suitable to a glittering evening then a seaside morning, and a great deal of overeating and heavy drinking. The only difference was that some of the very decorative girls there now emerged in smartly cut khaki drill when they changed out of their bikinis, and went off to do stints of duty at road-blocks in the mountains or to grace offices of the Party.

Hospitals in Christian sectors were far better than in the West, too. There was no shortage of drugs or necessary supplies, and more doctors and nurses were on duty, again because in general the majority of people in the medical professions were Christian. The best hospital in Lebanon, the American University Hospital, was in West Beirut and was still being run by an American administrator and a British Matron. But there was a terrible shortage of doctors: it was estimated that eighty per cent of those who had been practising in Beirut before the war had left. The nursing staff was sadly depleted too, mainly because girls could not get from their homes to the hospital. To compound all these difficulties, all semblance of authority had gone, so that when a group of commandoes brought in a wounded comrade they insisted that their man should be dealt with first and, to see that he was, often waved pistols about or pulled pins from grenades. When one wounded fighter died on the operating table, the surgeon hastily changed into his outdoor clothes and left the hospital by a back door. He was too afraid to tell the man's friends of the patient's death. 'They would have killed me in their first wave of emotion,' he said. Yet at times the American University Hospital was dealing with three hundred shrapnel wounds a day, though often the hard-pressed doctors and nurses could do no more than slap on a dressing and tell the victim to come back when things were quieter. They rarely were, so such people soon took to going to the emergency Field Hospital set up by the International Red Cross next to the Coral Beach Hotel. There, a polyglot mixture of young doctors helped by Swedish nurses operated in basic conditions similar to those in the movie *Mash* with the same mixture of professional expertise, cynicism and ribald humour.

The Coral Beach was also the headquarters of Dr Hassan Sabry al Kholy, the Arab League negotiator who shuttled untiringly between the warring sides, constantly seeking some new compromise. Dr Kholy never gave up and rarely lost his cool, but never really succeeded. Professional diplomat that he was, he knew quite well that his efforts were hopeless until President Assad and President Sadat decided the time had come to bring matters to a conclusion; until then, he went on doing what he could to minimize the carnage, organizing local ceasefires for specific purposes, reuniting families and, above all, keeping some kind of dialogue going. With Dr Kholy was the Commander of the Arab peace-keeping force, General Mohammed Ghonem, the Egyptian officer whose impossible task it was to try to impose order with a mere 2,500 troops. General Ghonem could do very little, but what was possible he and his men did. Their main achievement was to keep the Museum crossing point of the Green Line open for most of the time. There, Saudi or Sudanese soldiers in rotation held a 200-yard-long stretch of the highway on the Moslem side of the line, stoically maintaining their sentry posts even when mortars began falling around them, as they frequently did. To cross the line, one had to turn a sharp corner in the road which hid the opposing sides from each other, and whichever direction the traveller was going, it was always a reassuring sight to see the white-helmeted peace troops, few though they were, standing beside the road.

That bend in the road at the Museum crossing-place was the cause of a great deal of trouble, for each side, denied the possibility of direct observation, assumed the other was breaking whatever ceasefire happened to be in force at the time. The Mourabitoun held the sector on the Moslem side, and on the Christian side of the line different road-blocks within a few yards of each other were manned by tough, grizzled veteran fighters of the Syrian community, young N.L.P. militiamen, or regular Phalangist fighters. The Christians had a particular fear and animosity towards the Mourabitoun, and so under cover of darkness regularly opened up on their positions, eventually destroying the Sûreté National building, which was the most forward position on the Moslem side and was in fact being used by the Arab forces. So incensed was General Ghanem at this that he ordered the rubble, which was blocking the roadway, to be left where it was so that everyone could see that it was the Christians who had done the damage. Not that people had much doubt; the Palestinians were very much on the defensive by July and August, and had no intention of opening any new fronts if they could possibly avoid it. They were seeking a way out of the mess, not a means of prolonging it, in spite of all their bold words and such moves as a general mobilization. In fact, this was part of a plan by the moderate mainstream of the Resistance Movement to exert its control over all the dissident elements: Arafat had been told quite clearly by Syria that if he hoped to survive he must establish his authority – the Syrians would have preferred to replace him with Zuheir Mohsen, but had been reluctantly forced to accept that this was not possible. So the Syrian plan was that Fatah should become the dominant commando force, eventually, it was thought, able to impose its will on the small breakaway factions of the Rejection Front. The mobilization announced was seen as a step in that direction and at first was supposed to bring all those who were members of Rejection Front groups into the Fatah camp, but so violent were the behind-the-scenes objections from Habash and his allies that the plan had to be watered down, and the call-up was never really effective.

In the same way, on the Christian side the Syrians would have liked to see the Phalangists in complete command and again made their wishes plain. And the Phalangists did try to take over, not only because the Syrians wanted them to do so but also because they were concerned about the inroads being made by the N.L.P. in their strongholds in the Kesrouan. At one stage there was open warfare between the N.L.P. and the Phalangists with the N.L.P. office in Jounieh blown up and thirteen men killed in gun battles. After this there were talks between Chamoun and Gemayel to sort out their differences, which were much greater between the lower ranks than at the top; a general integration of the forces was decided upon, though the tension between Chamounists and Phalangists was always apparent when the two groups were in contact.

The third grouping on the Christian side might have been thought to present the greatest problem of all, as it was the most extreme; yet the Guardians of the Cedars were so fanatical that they attracted few recruits and never achieved any numerical strength, so that they could be dealt with at any time if it was felt necessary. The Guardians were run by a remarkable man who called himself Abou Arz (Father of the Cedars), though his real name was Etienne Sak'r and he came from Haifa, a fact he always tried to conceal. Sak'r was either slightly insane or so deliberately fanatical that he gave that impression. He was in the habit of saying that every Lebanese had a sacred duty to kill a Palestinian so that eventually all the 'foreign invaders' would be eliminated. He also set up a strange underground command post, would go about with his face masked even among his own supporters, and acted as if he were a general directing armies rather than the leader of a tiny and ineffectual splinter group.

Much more important and better concealed was something known merely as The Organization, a Maronite fraternal body which wielded great influence. It was in effect the lay arm of the Maronite monastic orders, which were headed by the doctrinaire Father Charbel Kassis, and in general followed the uncompromising line which the monks laid down. Their official position was that the Palestinians in Lebanon should be redistributed among all the Arab countries, so that the 'burden' of their presence would be spread to each country according to its ability. Unofficially, they propounded the theory that if life was made sufficiently difficult for the Palestinians in Lebanon, they would leave of their own accord and those who were left could easily be handled.

These extremist Christian groups were seen by some as the

equivalent of the Rejection Front organizations of the Palestinians, but they did not have the same kind of power, though they may have had the same influence. The Christian hard-liners got their way by argument and quiet pressure; the men of the Popular Front and its allies ensured themselves a place in the equation by force of arms. This difference was due not only to the relative strengths of the dissident groups but also to the very different way in which the Christians and Moslems were organized. On the Right, agreement between Chamoun and Gemayel ensured the strategic course of events, though tactical moves were left to local commanders. William Haoui had been the head of the Combined War Council, which directed operations by the Christian militias, and, when he was killed, his place was taken by Bachir Gemayel, whose brother Amin was in charge of the Metn district. In general, the Right was reasonably united, although it was the Franjiehs who controlled things in the North; at least their aims were roughly the same.

The Moslem side was much more fragmented. For a start, the alliance between the Palestinians and the Left-wing bloc led by Kamal Jumblatt was always a self-seeking affair with each party putting its own objectives before those of the whole. Jumblatt and his followers had as their main aim the reform of the Lebanese system on the lines they had laid down in their fourteen-point plan for a new political set-up in the country; they wanted proportional representation, an end to the assignment of Government posts on the basis of a man's religion, and a far more equitable distribution of the wealth available. It was hardly a revolutionary manifesto, yet it was sufficiently extreme in the Lebanese context to frighten the Moslem traditionalists, so that there was an immediate division between the old guard and the parties of the Left. In the same way, Jumblatt and his far-Left allies such as the Communists or Ba'athists had little in common. The Left-wing alliance had to rely on the Palestinians to provide its fighting strength, for few of the constituents of Jumblatt's bloc could command a really powerful militia. Jumblatt himself had always boasted of being able to put 'thousands' of armed and trained men into the field if need be, but in the event did not. At the beginning, only a small number of Jumblatt's supporters fought in the main battlefields of Beirut or Sidon, while most were kept standing by in the Chouf heartland, which saw very little action apart from some long-range exchanges around Jezzin. Eventually Jumblatt was forced by circumstances to announce the mobilization of all his Druze followers, though once again these seemed to be for defensive purposes. A few contingents were sent to the Metn front, which Jumblatt rightly described as the gateway to the Chouf, but they did little there and eventually withdrew in the face of Syrian and Phalangist pressure.

The one efficient and highly visible non-Palestinian group fighting on the Left was Ibrahim Kleilat's Mourabitoun, the Nasserite movement. When the war began, this force numbered only a few hundreds, but their successes quickly swelled the number and at the end they were one of the largest groups in Beirut, their sole theatre of operations. Apart from these relatively small militias, all the fighting was done by the Palestinians, and it was Fatah which effectively ran things and established what administrative services there were; Jumblatt set up rather pretentious committees, meant to be embryonic Ministries, but they were of little consequence with no power outside the Druze areas. It was Fatah which organized the minimal services available and eventually became the sole effective authority in Beirut, a situation not at all to the liking of many of the Moslem Lebanese living under this new Palestinian domination. In earlier years, the Palestinians in Lebanon had very clearly been second-class citizens; now, the situation was reversed and the Lebanese did not like it at all. It was very easy to find Moslems of all ages and classes living in West Beirut who were quite ready to speak of their growing disillusionment with the Palestinians. As the war went on, these people saw their own Lebanese objectives being subjugated to Palestinian aspirations, and gradually the unquestioning support which the Palestinians had received from Lebanese Moslems in the past turned first to grudging cooperation and then to outright hostility. It was not only that the Lebanese saw the Palestinians taking over their country and 'their' war, they were also appalled at many of the excesses of the commandoes. There was a segment of the population, mainly the younger, better-educated and more articulate people, who expected the Phalangists and Chamoun's N.L.P.

to behave badly, but had idealistic hopes that the cause of the Left and of Palestine would inspire better conduct. The brutal killings, the kidnappings, tortures and wilful savagery did a great deal to destroy what illusions were still held. It was the murder of one man, Khalil Salem, the Director of the Ministry of Finance, who was a member of the Greek Orthodox Church, which became the focus of this feeling. Salem was universally regarded as an incorruptible civil servant in a land where such men were rare; he was personally agreeable, did all he could for the welfare of his staff, and was largely responsible for keeping the monetary system in being, a remarkable feat in the anarchic conditions. Then he was abducted and murdered, apparently because he had agreed to transfer some of the funds held by the Central Bank to the East, to maintain the economy in the Christian areas, a very proper action for a patriot who was concerned to preserve some form of order so that eventually it would be possible to rebuild a united state. Salem's murder led to a new exodus of Christians from West Beirut and contributed towards the *de facto* partition which was daily becoming more apparent; it also did much to disillusion those few people who still believed the battle was between the good and the bad, right and wrong.

Inside the Resistance Movement the division was basically between Fatah and its moderate allies, and the Rejection Front led by George Habash and the Popular Front, though there were in fact dozens of other splits which were only gradually erased as the war progressed. At the beginning, half a dozen city streets on a confrontation line would be controlled by as many different factions, each demanding special authorization from anyone trying to move about there. The differences between the Left and the Palestinians, and among the commando groups, were exploited as hard as possible by the Syrians, who had a clear idea of what they wanted: Fatah to take control of the Resistance Movement and the Left, and the Phalangists to subdue Chamoun's party and the splinter groups. The Syrians believed that if these two parties were the dominant ones on their respective sides it would be easy to bring them together, for both were middle-of-the-road groups within their limitations and might be expected to reach some accommodation. In the event, this did not work, for both

Left and Right had subsidiary factions too powerful to be subjugated.

As the summer progressed, an atmosphere of fatalism seemed to overtake people. Despite all the talking and to-ing and fro-ing, nothing seemed to contribute towards ending the war, which was the everyday reality for all the people in the country – a number by now practically halved. Some 600,000 refugees had fled to Syria and there were 20,000 in Cyprus with Jordan, Egypt and a dozen other countries all acting as unwilling hosts to thousands more. The huge numbers of refugees caused serious problems: in Syria there were food and petrol shortages as a result of the influx, in Jordan prices were pushed upwards and accommodation became impossible to find, and in Cyprus the situation was so bad that the Government there began demanding visas from all Lebanese and insisted on each refugee producing a very substantial amount of cash before being allowed in. The trouble in Cyprus was that the island was only just recovering from its own war of 1974, still had a refugee problem, and could not handle the sudden demands made upon it, for Cyprus became the *entrepôt* for both Left and Right. Ships to and from Sidon and Tyre used the port of Limassol, while the flotilla of small boats linking Jounieh and the Christian area to the outside world had their home port in Larnaca. Both sides met arms dealers and financiers in Nicosia, where international agents of all sorts turned this small capital into an updated version of Lisbon in the 1940s.

In Beirut, still the centre of the battle, the people who were forced to remain there spent their lives in a daily fight for survival. With no electricity and no water, the hours were filled with the most basic demands of housekeeping as the women and children carted jerrycans of water up hundreds of stairs, made hazardous journeys into the streets in search of food, or sought out candles and paraffin lamps to cut down the long hours of darkness. As they did so, the random bombardment went on with shells and mortar bombs fired indiscriminately by both sides. There were the anomalies of a civil war too: telephone communication between East and West was usually possible, and the leaders of both sides kept in contact. At one time the Palestinians were urgently pressing the Christians to accept a gift of thousands of tons of diesel oil lying at the Zahrani refinery, controlled by the Left. The oil was badly needed for the Zouk Mikail power station, which supplied electricity to both parts of the divided city; but the Right were not eager to take the gift: they realized that sending the fuel north by tanker would free one of the few remaining undamaged tanks for storage of petrol, badly needed for the fighting vehicles of the Palestinians. Eventually they did take the fuel, and there was indeed an immediate relaxation in the chronic petrol shortage in West Beirut. Physical movements from one side to the other were also possible on most days, though it was always a hazardous trip and the crossing point was often closed by bombardment or sniper fire. Those who crossed regularly always carried petrol from East to West and at one time were returning with flour for the bakeries in the Rightist-held area. Those wishing to 'emigrate' permanently from one side to the other had to spend days getting permission from one or more of the warring groups: the Christians usually made little difficulty, for they seemed to want to rid their area of 'alien' elements, while the Palestinians were reluctant to see the Christians all leave, as they saw the propaganda advantage of holding up their sector as a model in which people of all religions could live amicably together. Because of these difficulties, foreign travellers, mainly journalists, who crossed frequently were much in demand as chauffeurs; they were usually known to the guards on both sides and were waved through with little trouble. But in the Lebanese way a few people could still arrange matters. Youssef Nazzal, the brilliant hotelier who kept the Carlton in West Beirut running at a profit throughout the war, had left his new Jaguar car in the Christian area. He telephoned the Phalangists in East Beirut, then Fatah in the West, and within hours his car was delivered. 'It cost me a great deal of money, but it was worth it,' he said.

There were regular, little-publicized political meetings too: Saeb Salam, seeking to exert his waning power, crossed from West to East to see what he could do; Bachir Gemayel left the Christian area to talk to Kamal Jumblatt; and the two chief Palestinian envoys, Hassan Salameh and Hani Hassan, met Alexander Gemayel almost weekly for inconclusive discussions of ways to end the conflict.

There were plenty of oddities to be noted as well. While mortars were falling in the Hamra area, an old gardener still went on clipping the bushes in front of the Reserve Bank; the sorely diminished water supplies were used to wash cars as well as people; in the shops and *souks* of both East and West fancy revolver holsters were among the fastest selling items – men of every age and class now all sported some kind of a gun at their belt. And strangest of all, the Lebanese Foreign Ministry in East Beirut continued to function. In the elegant marble halls of the Palais Bustros the diplomats chatted in French, carefully taking no notice of the disturbances outside, the frequent bursts of machine-gun fire or the crump of shells. With the Ministry in East Beirut and most Embassies in the western half of the city, there was little for the members of the staff to do, but they turned up each day, impeccably dressed, and continued to write their memoranda, to discuss possible appointments and perhaps on a good day even to receive a visit from the Papal Nuncio, who had moved to the Christian sector. The position was complicated further by a dispute over who the Minister was: Philippe Takla was Foreign Minister in Rashid Karami's six-man 'rescue' cabinet, but as he soon left the country and showed no signs of returning, President Franjieh announced his dismissal and gave the portfolio to Camille Chamoun. Karami claimed this was unconstitutional and illegal, which gave the suave gentlemen at the Palais scope for some splendid recondite arguments with much delving into past diplomatic history and practice.

While Beirut was suffering and surviving, big changes were going on in the south of the country. The area along the Israeli frontier was relatively untouched by the war, as the two or three Christian villages in this predominantly Shia district were able to live at peace with their Moslem neighbours until towards the end of 1976. They did suffer, however, for all normal services disappeared, the few doctors who had practised in this neglected region left, there were severe food shortages and the farmers could no longer sell their produce. It was too good a chance for the Israelis to miss. First they announced they would provide medical treatment for anyone needing it and established special clinics close to the border. This necessitated gates in the high wire-link fence which had been built to keep the commandoes out; the open gates needed protection, so new forts were built right on the frontier; and to ensure order, Israeli troops had to go into Lebanese territory on regular patrols. Next came Israeli offers of employment, eagerly accepted by people from the Christian village of Rmeich. It was the Israelis, too, who now bought the tobacco which had formerly been sent to the Lebanese Régie. Soon the South was completely dominated and controlled by Israel, just as the Akkar and the Bekaa were under Syrian 'protection'; the 'cantonization' of Lebanon was a fact.

12

The slow
but dreadful end

On the battlefronts, things were coming to their slow but
dreadful end. All attention was focused on Tal Zaatar, because
it was the symbol to both sides of the Palestinians' will to fight
on, but there was pressure too on Nabaa, while in the mountains the Phalangists were sending in reinforcements ready to
expel the Fatah and Jumblatt troops from their positions on
the bare hills around Sannin. In Beirut the regular exchanges
of artillery and mortar fire continued, and in the bustling new
Christian capital of Jounieh shells often fell in the harbour or
along the waterfront even as people were water-skiing in the
bay. In Sidon, Lebanese Arab Army men had to go into action
to prevent arms shipments being hijacked by men of the Rejection Front, the Israelis regularly stopped and searched boats
going into this last remaining Left-held port, and in Tripoli
men of the Zghorta Liberation Army had been joined by Phalangist contingents as the siege of the city was tightened – the
Syrians were to the north, so nothing could be taken in that
way, and supplies could reach the defenders only by sea.

On all sides now there was a general recognition that the
war was coming to an end, though it was still not clear whether
there would be total military victory for the Right, or if a political solution could be found before the Phalangists and their
allies overran the last Palestinian strongholds. Very aware of
the diminishing time in which to salvage something from the
wreckage, President Sadat and the feudal Gulf Rulers were
striving desperately to find some diplomatic formula which
would allow them a say in the shape of the final settlement.
The Egyptian leader paid a visit to King Khaled of Saudi
Arabia and they announced plans for a new summit conference; Dr Kholy continued his valiant efforts, while Syria

171

still seemed to be relying on its troops and its *carte blanche* from the West to bring things to an end. Finally, it was military power which tipped the balance: the Right with Syrian permission and encouragement decided to eliminate the Palestinian enclaves in East Beirut by force of arms. They had hoped to avoid being forced to put in final assaults on Nabaa and Tal Zaatar, as they realized that they would be bound to suffer heavy casualties; starving the defenders out would have been much simpler, but after seven weeks neither place showed any sign of giving in.

Both enclaves had taken a terrible battering. Nabaa, inhabited largely by Shia workers who had migrated to Beirut from Baalbeck and the South, was a suburb of high-rise apartment buildings with squatters' makeshift shelters in between, and, as it had a defensible perimeter formed by roads all round, it was no easy place to take. Three or four times the Phalangists had announced its capture, for Nabaa was the particular target of Amin Gemayel's men, whose headquarters were not far away at Jdeide. Each time, the Palestinian defenders had replied with new bursts of firing and salvoes from their heavy weapons. It could not go on; day after day the Christian attackers poured in their devastating fire, under no compulsion to conserve stocks, which were arriving regularly at Tabarja Beach, most of them now coming in ships maintaining a shuttle service between Lebanon and Israel. Day and night the Phalangists nibbled away at the Palestinian defences, taking a blockhouse here, a machine-gun post there, a protective building the next time. Finally, on 6 August, the last assault was mounted: after hours of softening up, the Phalangists stormed in, easily beating the rearguard attempts to hold the place. They were helped, too, by the surrender of some of those supposed to be organizing the defence: three of the Shia leaders went over to the Right, leaving their people alone and isolating the Palestinians who were still fighting. This last-minute defection followed a change of sides by the two main Shia leaders, Kamal Assad, the House Speaker, and the Imam Moussa Sad'r, previously bitter opponents. Both Assad and Sad'r had paid frequent visits to Damascus, and were concerned at the Syrian occupation of the Bekaa, where many of their people lived, and about the Israeli hold on the South. The charitable explanation was that the two men decided to throw in their lot with the Syrians, and implicitly with the Right, in an effort to save the lives of the people of their community; whatever the reason, their change of heart was obvious and the result was that the heads of the Shia community in Nabaa felt able to follow suit. It was this, according to the Palestinians, which brought the sudden collapse after the long defence of the area, though it was clear that the strong attacking forces would have prevailed within days even if the shift in allegiance had not occurred.

If it was, in fact, easier to take Nabaa than the Right originally expected, this did not decrease the savagery shown to the Palestinian fighters there: they were massacred to a man, the few who came out from behind barricades with their hands up were gunned down without mercy. But in what seemed a careful policy, and a significant realization of what was going on among the Moslem parties, the ordinary people of Nabaa, the Shia, were rarely harmed – indeed, the Phalangists went out of their way to help them and within a week of the fall of the suburb the first families who had fled were brought back, escorted by Shia police officers from Baalbeck, and were helped to find accommodation and food by the Phalangists. It was the Palestinians alone who felt the fury of the Right in Nabaa, and it was a fury which even extended beyond death: bodies of Palestinian fighters were propped up at street corners, and Phalangists took cheerful pot-shots at the cadavers as they looted the houses and apartments. Other dead Palestinians were hitched to cars or trucks and towed through the Christian areas as final convincing proof that this time claims to have captured Nabaa were accurate; one body at least was dragged behind a car all the way from Nabaa to the ravine above Jounieh which was regularly used as an execution ground and mass grave. Crowds along the route cheered as the Phalangist militiamen in the car hooted and waved while they swerved in and out of the traffic with their grisly burden behind them.

The correct treatment of the Shia was intended to deepen the rifts in the Moslem community, and it succeeded. The Shia living in the Bekaa Valley were impressed by the Syrian-imposed order there, while those in the south of the country were forced to look more to the Israelis for help and protection than to their own people. The acceptance by the Imam and by Kamal Assad of the Syrian–Rightest alliance put paid to the Sunni–Druze–Shia bloc which Jumblatt and his partners had hoped to forge, as well as whittling away the power of the traditional Sunni leaders, who had to have the support of other Moslem groups if they were to make an effective comeback.

The fall of Nabaa left only one Palestinian enclave in East Beirut: Tal Zaatar, one of the oldest and biggest refugee camps in the country, at one time inhabited by 30,000 people with its own poverty belt of poor Lebanese, Kurds, and Southern Shia camped on its perimeter. Tal Zaatar had been established in 1948, when the first refugees fled from Palestine, and had grown ever since to the dismay of the Christians in the surrounding suburbs and the fear of others who owned the factories around its shanty-town core. Like many other camps, it contained multi-storey buildings as well as tin shacks, it had its own hospitals, clinics, schools, mosques and churches – even a prison – and it was divided into sectors where people who came from the same areas of Palestine again huddled together, and where different factions of the Resistance Movement were in control. Thus the highest point in the camp was known as General Command Hill, because Jabril's men were in charge there, while in other places Fatah, the Popular Front, the P.D.F.L.P. and Saiqa all had their offices and their spheres of influence. Saiqa, by the beginning of August, was no longer an organized force within the camp, though its offices had not been taken over violently as the premises of the Syrian-backed commandoes elsewhere had been. In Tal Zaatar there was a far greater sense of camaraderie than there was outside, and the Saiqa men had in fact gone on fighting on the Palestinian side even after Syrian regular forces had gone into action against the Palestinians in Lebanon. Only gradually did the Saiqa men give up, sometimes as a result of the news filtering through on the transistor radios of what was going on, and later following direct orders, for there was a regular Syrian force in Tal Zaatar and its commander had authority over the Saiqa men. This Syrian unit was comprised of twenty-five officers and soldiers who manned the anti-aircraft guns mounted in the camp to protect it against Israeli air raids; soon after the siege began el Fatah gunners took over from the Syrians, who did not try to resist in a situation where they did not have enough men to put up a fight. After that the Syrians gradually made their way out; it was Saiqa men who in the last days organized the desperate parties of half-starved men, women and children that made the perilous journey through the perimeter defences to give themselves up to the besieging Christians.

From July onwards the position of the camp was critical. It was shelled day and night, and major attacks were launched by the Right on more than sixty occasions; all were beaten back, though eye-witness evidence showed that the assaults were less formidable than the Christians reported: if one or two of the attackers was killed or wounded, this was usually the signal for the attempt to gain ground to be called off with all the attackers involved escorting their slain or wounded comrades back to the starting place. The most effective weapon the Right had was the blockade of Tal Zaatar; the total inability of the Palestinians to send in a relief column or even to infiltrate individuals from the middle of June onwards meant that conditions in the camp became nearly unbearable. In the end it was the lack of food, medicines, sanitation and water which brought about the fall of the camp as much as the pounding from the Rightist artillery. Water was the most difficult problem of all: there were some wells, but they were dreadfully polluted, so that everyone still there soon had dysentery; and day after day, as the ring was tightened, another well would become too dangerous to use. A huge mass grave was used for the bodies, which were buried under cover of darkness with one of the sheikhs still there chanting the *Koran* in a whisper so that the sound would not draw fire. Food consisted mainly of rice or beans boiled on paraffin stoves in the basements of apartment blocks and factories where the people spent all their time. Over everything, there was the stench: the smell of death, of unwashed bodies, of ordure. Tal Zaatar, never a pleasant or a pretty place, was at this time as close to a hell on earth as it was possible for anywhere to become, and its inhabitants believed they could look forward only to death as a release.

This was not, in fact, the only prospect: the Right was willing to allow Tal Zaatar to be evacuated, for they wanted to get rid of this thorn in the side of the Christian East of Beirut rather than to score a huge victory at tremendous cost. Arafat and his lieutenants considered the possibilities. If they agreed to the urgent appeals of the Red Cross and of Dr Kholy for the total evacuation of the camp, they would get some 300 of their trained fighters back, though the weapons would have to be left behind. Hundreds, perhaps thousand of people would be saved from death and would come flooding in to West Beirut, where they would be a liability, not a gain. On the debit side, too, was the effect which a voluntary evacuation of the camp would have: Tal Zaatar had become the symbol of Palestinian resistance, of steadfastness in the face of failure. If it were abandoned, the psychological effect would be catastrophic. The decision they made seemed to Arafat and Salah Khalaf, his second in command, to be obvious, and to be obviously right, so the message went over the crackling radio to the camp: fight on.

This was not enough; every possible propaganda advantage had to be gained, so after days and weeks of delay the Fatah commanders agreed that the Red Cross should at least be allowed to bring out the most seriously wounded people from the camp. Jean Hoefliger, the chief Red Cross representative in Lebanon, had been able to make a reconnaissance expedition to the camp under the cover of a local ceasefire, and he was confident that the wounded could be evacuated if a truce could be arranged. Conscious of the danger to the people who would have to go in with him, Hoefliger was determined to get firm guarantees before risking his men, and so began the weary business of trying to get agreement from all sides. The Palestinians, having made their decision, were eager for the matter to go ahead, though all the various groups had to be contacted to see that they accepted the decision taken by Arafat and Khalaf. Then it was the turn of the Right, and there things were more complicated. The man supposed to be in command of the forces besieging Tal Zaatar was Commandant Fuad Malek, a burly, jolly Christian officer of the Lebanese Army who had sided with the Right when the Army broke up. He was quite agreeable to the evacuation plan and proclaimed himself eager to conduct operations in accordance with all the rules of war; so long as the Palestinians did not make use of any truce to improve their positions, he was prepared to agree, he said. But Commandant Malek was by no means the only one involved. The largest sector around the camp was held by militiamen of Chamoun's N.L.P., who in theory were commanded by Chamoun's son Dany, though in fact it was Maroun Khoury, a well-known local gangster, who actually ran things. Dany Chamoun would agree to a truce, but would the men there do as they were told? It was a question which Hoefliger and his men eventually had to put to the test. A third force was also involved: the Phalangists held a sector at Dekwaneh through Harikat, one of their subsidiary organizations. So Bachir Gemayel and 'Joseph', the Phalangist commander on the spot, also had to be contacted.

After some false starts, the Red Cross convoy was at last permitted to begin work. A dozen trucks driven by Armenians went in, led by Hoefliger in a car, smoking a thin cheroot as usual. Before the lorries were allowed to move, the N.L.P. militiamen searched each one and removed all first aid kits, any cans of water, and the packets of sandwiches the drivers had with them. Even at this late stage, the blockade was the most important weapon the attackers had. When the convoy reached the football field on the perimeter of the defended area, Swiss and Arab Red Cross workers, men and women, staked out a collection zone with the international organization's flags, and slowly the operation got under way with the wounded being brought down by the Palestinians in the camp and handed to the Red Cross workers, who then loaded them on to the lorries. Shooting went on in the upper part of the camp while the evacuation was in progress despite all the assurances given by both sides, though nothing happened too close to the football field, and things went fairly smoothly. It was as the convoy drove away from Tal Zaatar that the real trouble came, for it had to be checked by both the N.L.P. and the Phalangists; one of the Christian gunmen recognized a known Palestinian leader among the wounded. The man had his arm in plaster and there was a blood-stain on his shoulder, but the militiamen were not satisfied: they wanted to take the Palestinian away and have him examined by their own doctor, and would not allow the trucks through until this was done. Somehow, Hoefliger persuaded the Rightists to give way, helped by the very obvious divisions between the N.L.P., the Army and the Phalangists, which at one stage led to an exchange of fire. One of the best kept secrets, for it would have ruined any chances of repeating the operation, was that the Palestinian commander was in fact completely unhurt; he quietly disappeared as soon as the convoy reached the safety of West Beirut and his wife, who had been with him in the camp, also calmly made her way to safety when the mass exodus took place. In Moslem West Beirut, the first returning heroes of Tal Zaatar were greeted with vast enthusiasm, with volleys of gunfire and cheering crowds more fitted to the return of conquerors than the evacuation of wounded fighters from an impossible position; as usual, Palestinian propaganda was making a victory out of a disaster.

On two other occasions the Red Cross was able to go into Tal Zaatar to bring out injured, though it was much more hazardous on the third occasion with the Red Cross men themselves the target of sniper fire from an N.L.P. militiaman: a driver was wounded and one of the people being brought out of the camp was hit a second time. So bad was the situation then that the Red Cross efforts were suspended, and events moved so fast that they never had a chance to resume.

The stories brought out of the camp by those evacuated painted a terrifying picture of what was going on, and of the hopelessness of the position. A Swedish nurse, Eva Stahl, who had been married to a Palestinian killed in the camp and who was herself terribly wounded, was the most articulate of those brought out. She spoke of the Palestinians' determination to fight to the end, of the shortages of food and water, the lack of medical supplies and the terrible strain of living under constant bombardment. Even as she was telling her story, messages were being sent from the camp to the leaders of the Resistance asking for permission to surrender; the fighters in the camp, abandoned by most of their commanders, realized they were beaten and wanted to save what lives they could. At their headquarters in Beirut, Arafat and his war council would not hear of it; they were still determined to extract the maximum propaganda advantage at a time when the Palestinian cause badly needed a boost. Day after day they sent back the simple message 'Fight on'. Hoefliger, who had been into the camp himself, knew the situation better than most and, with Dr Kholy, was doing all he could to get a ceasefire which would allow the evacuation of women and children – on the last occasion the Red Cross went in, the Palestinians in the camp had to use their rifle butts to beat back unwounded people trying to scramble aboard the Red Cross lorries. And each night dozens of people made the hazardous trip through an orange grove in the Dekwaneh sector, usually led by Saiqa men, to give themselves up to the Phalangists there. Even at this desperate juncture, few would risk trying to surrender to Chamoun's militiamen; they had a very short way with Palestinians of any kind.

Hoefliger's efforts did have some success, though just how much was in dispute right up to the last moment: for when the final day came, some Palestinians claimed there had been an agreement to allow the peaceful evacuation of the camp and that the Christians attacked just two hours before the operation was to begin. Fuad Malek said simply, 'What agreement?' and, when told that Bachir Gemayel had agreed to a truce, the N.L.P. militia commander, Dany Chamoun, sneered, 'And how big a front does he hold? Eighty yards!' Other Palestinians agreed that there had been no truce and claimed that the Christians had tricked their men into giving up by driving up in an ambulance to give the impression that another Red Cross operation was about to begin. Whatever the truth of the matter, the end came for Tal Zaatar at 6 a.m. on Thursday 12 August. And though the war dragged on for another three months, this date marked the military victory of the Right, supported by the Syrians, and the end of the reluctant Palestinian attempts to take over the Lebanese State.

And a bloody end it was. After one of the most intensive softening-up barrages yet used, the Right-wing forces stormed in as thousands of men, women and children tried to get out, brushing past Palestinians still firing from their perimeter strong-points. Fuad Malek, the Army commander directing the Christian operation, claimed that his men had behaved 'as soldiers, most correctly', and said he had not allowed the N.L.P. militiamen to go into the camp until his men had gone through it to subdue oppositon and secure the place. If this was true, it made the situation even worse, for Tal Zaatar was the scene of one of the worst massacres of the war perpetrated by either side. As the attackers stormed in, anyone they saw was mown down, which was not surprising, for in an attack on a packed maze of streets men of the assault force could never be sure where they were or who they would meet around the next corner: the natural tendency was to shoot as soon as a movement was seen. Hundreds died in this way and hundreds more were killed by shelling, and more still as they tried to flee the camp. Whole families were found lying dead within yards of each other in front of their shanty homes, gunned down as they tried to escape the onslaught. According to the estimates of the N.L.P. commanders themselves, some 1,200 people were killed during the storming of the camp and the barrage that preceded it; and at least another 800 were 'executed' in the hours after the camp was taken. The N.L.P. men made no apology for this; in such a war, it was expected. They merely congratulated themselves that this time their excesses were not shown on the television screens of the world. 'You see', said one Christian officer, 'we learnt from Maslakh. This time you didn't see anything, did you?'

Those who went into the camp within hours of its fall saw enough: bodies everywhere, men, women and children; looters so eager to get into the place to seize the little that these refugees had managed to amass that they drove over bodies lying in the way, until several at the main entrance looked like cartoon cat figures, flattened and spread out on the bare ground. The N.L.P. men quarrelled among themselves over the spoils, frequently letting off their rifles to protect a particularly rewarding place they had found – they spread the idea that snipers were still active to try to discourage others from joining in the fun. For some people, it was all too much: one brave fighter strode to seek his rewards, laughing and pointing at the corpses all around. As he rounded a corner he almost stepped on the body of an old man who had been caught by a burst right across his body: the stench was awful, the guts were spilling out. This bold looter turned away vomiting and gave up his hope of riches.

Dr Kholy lost his cool for the first time over Tal Zaatar:

on the Wednesday afternoon he had been trying to arrange a truce, and was in the N.L.P. command post at the edge of the camp talking to Fuad Malek and other officers as the barrage went on – a barrage watched by Colonel Aly Madani, the Syrian liaison officer also supposed to be working for a cease-fire. Dr Kholy saw some of the prisoners taken at the camp being rounded up and, by dint of one of those outbursts of controlled rage which even the most suave diplomat can turn on, he managed to get fifty of them released into his care. Dr Kholy brought them back to West Beirut personally: only then was it realized that most of them were Syrians who would have been freed anyway. Fuad Malek did keep some Palestinian prisoners and Amin Gemayel also claimed to have some: Commandant Malek allowed people to see those he took and gave their names to the Red Cross. Amin Gemayel's prisoners were never seen and no names were ever disclosed; if there were any, they had short shrift, like most of those taken in the camp. Mass murder was the order of the day there, and even those who managed to get out and make their way on foot to the West were not safe: a group of ten Palestinian nurses was stopped by N.L.P. men, lined up and shot. A Palestinian doctor with them escaped because months before he had treated one of the N.L.P. militiamen involved, who repaid the debt by letting him go.

By mid-afternoon on that Thursday, Jean Hoefliger had managed to organize a convoy to bring the people still milling about near the camp to the safety of the Moslem West. As they drove through the Green Line, there were jeers from the Christian victors and, when they got to the West of the city, there was none of the welcoming gun-fire which had greeted the first wounded to be brought out of the camp. At long last, the Palestinians and their Lebanese allies realized what a defeat they had suffered. The Palestinian leaders had grasped the situation much earlier: they saw that they were denied the final propaganda advantage they had hoped to get by the escape of so many thousands, while the massacre of the rest and the fall of the camp was an event which would be taken as a huge Right-wing victory by every Arab. In their bitterness the Palestinian commanders ordered their artillery to open up on the fringes of the camp with the ostensible objective of hampering the attackers and helping those inside; instead the shells were landing among the hundreds who had got through the perimeter and were trying to escape. When they were told of this, the Palestinians made no attempt to lift their fire: they wanted martyrs.

The fall of Tal Zaatar marked the end for the Palestinians in the military sense. A month or so later, when the Phalangists and Syrians took over the mountain positions on Sannin, in Ain Tourah and in Metn without opposition, it was merely a tidying up operation, underlining an established fact. The Palestinians would have had to evacuate these exposed outposts as soon as the snows came, so the Right-wing advance before that happened was no more than a demonstration of what could be done, a muscle-flexing exercise. In Tripoli and Beirut, the two sides held their positions, and had regular exchanges of artillery fire and mortars; but it was a desultory business now with neither Right nor Left trying to advance. Both sides were conscious that for all practical purposes the war was over and were content to minimize casualties in the final few weeks.

The political end came not in Lebanon but in Saudi Arabia: on 18 October, after careful preparation and a lot of behind-the-scenes horse-trading, President Sadat and President Assad met in Riyadh. Yasser Arafat and Elias Sarkis were there too, plus the Saudis and Kuwaitis who had arranged the whole thing. The fact that the bargaining had been completed in advance and that this was more a public relations exercise than a negotiating session was shown in the way the Presidents, who had been at each other's throats for months past, now cheerfully posed for photographers, smiling, shaking hands, chatting amicably. Arafat, hovering on the fringes of the picture, knew that it was all over: no matter how brave the words of the Palestinians were or their actions, agreement between the two leading Arab States meant that the Resistance Movement had no chance of going its own way. The Saudis and Kuwaitis, as usual, had made it all possible by judicious use of their millions: Syria, tottering under the economic impact of its involvement in Lebanon and cut off from one of its main sources of revenue by Iraq's refusal to use it for transit of oil, was promised cheap loans and immediate grants; Egypt, chronically in need of finance for the ambitious development projects which might one day enable it to achieve economic take-off, was offered new aid; and the Palestinians in the form of Arafat and the P.L.O. would be supported if they behaved. Egypt in return drew back slightly from its commitment to the West by announcing the resumption of 'a political dialogue' with Russia, an involved way of saying that the military option was still available in dealings with Israel and that Syria would not necessarily have to go it alone in seeking the restoration of its conquered territory. Syria halted the advance its troops had begun in Lebanon for preparations to be made for a negotiated occupation of the battle-grounds to avoid further losses. Elias Sarkis undertook to see that the Right in Lebanon would not seek to exploit its victory, and that his régime would institute the reforms which everyone agreed were necessary: basically he formally assented to Syrian overlordship. And the Palestinians – the defeated Palestinians in the person of Yasser Arafat were there to be spoken to, not to speak. Yet Arafat himself did salvage something, for the Syrians had wanted him out, rightly seeing his style of diplomacy as their main stumbling-block in establishing total overall control of the Movement. President Sadat would not agree; he realized that Arafat was not only the international symbol of the commandoes, the respectable face of the *fedayeen*, but also the one man able to maintain moderate control and perhaps to stop the extremists taking over or mounting the wild international terrorist campaign they had threatened if they were beaten in Lebanon.

So in the end everyone got something out of the Riyadh meeting, whose terms were quickly ratified by a summit conference in Cairo. There, the main 'decision' (for in fact it was merely a question of rubber-stamping what had already been agreed) was to send a 30,000-strong Arab peace-keeping force to Lebanon with President Sarkis free to choose which countries would furnish the troops needed, and with Sarkis as the nominal Commander-in-Chief. Asked which States Sarkis was likely to approach, one of the more cynical and better-informed diplomats in Cairo gave the game away: 'Syria, Syria, and Syria,' he said. And he was right. When the war was brought to an end on 15 November, it was the Syrians who took over Beirut, always the heart of the problem, with a few minor contingents from Saudi Arabia, Sudan, Abu Dhabi and Libya tagging along to give an air of respectable pan-Arabism.

So, after one year, seven months and fifteen days, the Lebanese civil war came to an end and an army of occupation took over. The Syrians not only dismantled the barricades and established a 600-yard-wide corridor between Christian and Moslem halves of Beirut, they also took control of such key points as the radio station, the Ministry of Information, the Central Bank and Army headquarters. The fighters on both sides moved out of their positions and, for the first time in months, changed into civilian clothes and left their guns at home. Ironically, it was the beaten Palestinians who greeted the Syrians as saviours, not conquerors, for they believed that at the very least Syrian occupation would ensure an Arab future for Lebanon, rather than a special position as a European outpost in the Middle East. The Christians, who should have been grateful, welcomed the men who had come to their help in their hour of sorest trouble with scowls and suspicion. Too late they realized that they were exchanging one army of occupation for another – and a much bigger and more efficient one at that.

The ordinary Lebanese, Moslem or Christian, rich or poor, who had suffered so much for so long, could only rejoice. Within hours of the almost bloodless Syrian take-over of Beirut enterprising street traders from both sides of the line had set up their barrows outside the Museum, once the sole hazardous link between the two sides. Traffic reappeared on the streets, shop-keepers began sorting out their premises, and families who had been cooped up in their homes ventured out to gape at the devastation all about them; suddenly there was authority again, and it was the most wonderful thing the Lebanese had seen in nineteen months. Peace, everyone knew, brought with it plenty of problems; but after the long months of war, the random terror, the kidnappings and killings, the 44,000 dead and 180,000 injured, the destruction of a city, a country, and a way of life – after all that, peace was enough. Lebanese and Palestinians alike swore that never again would they allow politics, bigotry or factional advantage to lead them to the abyss. At the time, they meant it.

Leading figures
in the war

Sharif AKHAOUI — Radio announcer famous for telling the truth when no-one else would.

Yasser ARAFAT — Chairman of the P.L.O., leader of el Fatah, and the overall Palestinian commander who had a reputation as a moderate.

Hafez ASSAD — President of Syria.

Kamal ASSAD — Speaker of the Lebanese Parliament and a traditional leader of the Shia Moslems.

Rifaat ASSAD — Brother of President Assad; he commanded the Syrian special forces.

Camille CHAMOUN — Former President and leader of the Right-wing National Liberal Party.

Dany CHAMOUN — Son of Camille Chamoun and commander of the N.L.P. militia.

Fuad CHEHAB — Former Lebanese Army commander and President who extricated the country from an earlier civil war.

Suleiman FRANJIEH — President of Lebanon from 1970 until September 1976, a Right-wing extremist whose stubborn retention of office helped to prolong the crisis.

Tony FRANJIEH — Son of the President, commander of the Zghorta Liberation Army and a Minister with a reputation for corruption in two governments.

Amin GEMAYEL — Son of Sheikh Pierre Gemayel and commander of the Right-wing forces in the Metn district.

Bachir GEMAYEL	Son of Sheikh Pierre Gemayel and commander of all the Right-wing military forces.
Pierre GEMAYEL	Leader of the Phalangist Party, the main group on the Right.
Mohammed GHONEM	Egyptian general who commanded the original small Arab peace-keeping force.
George HABASH	Leader of the Popular Front for the Liberation of Palestine, an extremist commando group.
Nayef HAWATMEH	Leader of the Popular Democratic Front for the Liberation of Palestine, an extremist commando group.
Ahmed JABRIL	Leader of the Popular Front–General Command, a small but powerful commando group.
Abdul Salam JALLOUD	Libyan Prime Minister who tried to mediate in Lebanon.
Kamal JUMBLATT	Feudal millionaire landowner who led the Left-wing alliance in Lebanon.
Rashid KARAMI	Leading Sunni Moslem politician and frequent Prime Minister of Lebanon who held that office for most of the war.
Charbel KASSIS	Priest who headed the Maronite monastic orders whose advice had great influence on Right-wing policy.
Salah KHALAF	Deputy to Arafat and one-time head of Black September.
Hassan Sabry al KHOLY	Arab League diplomat who acted as mediator during most of the war.
Ibrahim KLEILAT	Leader of the Mourabitoun, the Nasserite militia which did much of the fighting for the Left in Beirut.
Zuheir MOHSEN	Head of Saiqa, the Syrian-backed commando organization.

Maarouf SA'AD	Mayor of Sidon whose death in a riot marked the beginning of the civil war.
Anwar SADAT	President of Egypt.
Moussa SAD'R	Spiritual head of the Shia community in Lebanon who championed the cause of the poor but eventually defected to Syria.
Etienne SAK'R	Also known as Abou Arz, strange leader of the Right-wing extremist Guardians of the Cedars.
Saeb SALAM	Leading Sunni Moslem politician and a former Lebanese Prime Minister.

Abbreviations

A.L.F.	The Arab Liberation Front: the Iraqi-backed commando group.
A.N.M.	The Arab Nationalist Movement: the far-Left political party founded by George Habash.
N.L.P.	The National Liberal Party: the Right-wing party led by Camille Chamoun.
P.A.S.C.	The Palestine Armed Struggle Command: the military police of the resistance movement.
P.D.F.L.P.	The Popular Democratic Front for the Liberation of Palestine: a Left-wing commando group which broke away from Habash's Popular Front.
P.F.L.P.	The Popular Front for the Liberation of Palestine: the extremist commando group led by George Habash.
P.F.L.P.–G.C.	The Popular Front for the Liberation of Palestine – General Command: a small breakaway commando group led by Ahmed Jabril.
P.L.A.	The Palestine Liberation Army: the 'regular forces' of the resistance movement.
P.L.O.	The Palestine Liberation Organization: the umbrella body linking most organizations in the resistance movement.
U.N.	The United Nations.
U.N.W.R.A.	The United Nations Works and Relief Agency for Palestinian Refugees.

Index

189

INDEX

Palestine Red Crescent, 49
Palestinians, refugee camps in Lebanon,
2–3, 4, 43–4, 48, 55; and 1969 Cairo
agreement, 55–6; early clashes with
Phalangists, 25; and causes of civil
war, 4, 67; Syria's objectives towards,
5; aid from Iraq, 7; threaten to blow
up Murr Tower, 15; commando raids
on Israel, 25–6, 46; Israel's retaliation
against, 27–8, 68–9; battle at Kfar
Chouba, 28–9; fighting in Sidon, 34–
6, 37; massacre in Ain Rumaneh, 37–
40; aims in civil war, 41–2; establish
commando bases in refugee camps, 44;
growth of resistance movement, 44, 47;
Battle of Karameh, 47–8; establish
bases in the Arkoub, 48; Lebanese
Army moves against, 53–4, 71–2; and
exclusion of Phalangists from Cabinet,
79; destruction of Souk Tawile, 87–8;
besiege Zahle, 92–3; arms supplies, 94–
5, 111, 143; Army drives out of hotels,
99; Phalangists besiege in Tal Zaatar,
101–2; Damour front, 102–3, 105; air
attacks, 103–4; communications system, 104; attack Army at Khalde, 104;
and first Syrian intervention, 107, 108;
and Assad's northern alliance, 111;
and Franjieh's programme of national
reform, 116; and Ahdab's attempted
coup, 122; capture Holiday Inn, 124–
5; advance into mountains, 126; possible conflict with Syria, 126–7, 131;
arms supplies blockaded by Syria, 133,
140; and Syrian invasion, 143, 144,
145–7, 149, 150–2; Jalloud tries to save
from total subjugation, 152–3; welcome peace-keeping troops, 155; Phalangists continue to attack in camps,
156–7; and American evacuation, 157;
and partition of Beirut, 158; resistance
movement tries to control dissidents,
162; alliance with Jumblatt, 164;
Moslem disillusionment with, 165–6;
factions in resistance movement, 166–
7; lose Nabaa, 172–3; and siege of Tal
Zaatar, 174–82; and end of civil war,
1, 8, 182, 183
Palm Beach Hotel, 23–4, 93
Phalangists, aims, 4; early clashes with
Palestinians, 25, 53–4, 60–1; and start
of civil war, 75, 76–7; arms supplies, 7,
94, 95; battle for Kantari, 13, 15–16,
22–3; try to involve Army in civil war,
18, 36–7; destroy *souk* area of Beirut,
18, 19, 87; massacre in Ain Rumaneh,
37–40; Jumblatt tries to exclude from
Cabinet, 75–6, 79; revenge for Fanar
murders, 97; lose control of hotels,
98, 124; and possible partition of
Lebanon, 99; besiege Tal Zaatar, 101–
2, 177–8, 179; destroy Karantina and
Maslakh, 104–5; and Syrian intervention, 131, 145, 150; and partition of
Beirut, 139; continue to attack camps,
155; try to take command of
Christians, 162–3; fight in mountains,
171; besiege Tripoli, 171; and battle for
Nabaa, 172–3; and end of civil war, 1,
8, 182; *see also* Christians
Phoenicia Hotel, 94, 98, 125
Police Judiciaire, 85
Popular Democratic Front for the
Liberation of Palestine (P.D.F.L.P.),
60, 71, 174
Popular Front for the Liberation of
Palestine (P.F.L.P.), 51, 58–9, 60–1,
140, 164, 166, 174
Popular Front for the Liberation of
Palestine – General Command, 39, 59–
60, 134–5
Popular Security Forces, 139, 158–9
Portugal, 95
Post Office, 63–4, 100–1
Progressive Socialist Party, 59, 75
Proteine Ltd, 30–1

Qubeiyat, 119, 142, 143, 144–5

Rachaya, 55, 119–20
Radio Lebanon, 90–1
Radio Orient, 104
Ramullah, 43
Raouche, 92
Ras Nakoura, 120
Rayek airbase, 149
Red Cross, 161, 176, 177–8, 179, 181
Rejection Front, 39, 40, 95, 123, 137, 140,
147, 158, 162, 164, 166, 171
Reuters, 12
Riad, Mahmoud, 41, 131, 157
Rifai, Nureddin, 70, 79, 80, 81
Riyadh, 138, 182–3
Rmeich, 7, 170
Rumania, 95

195

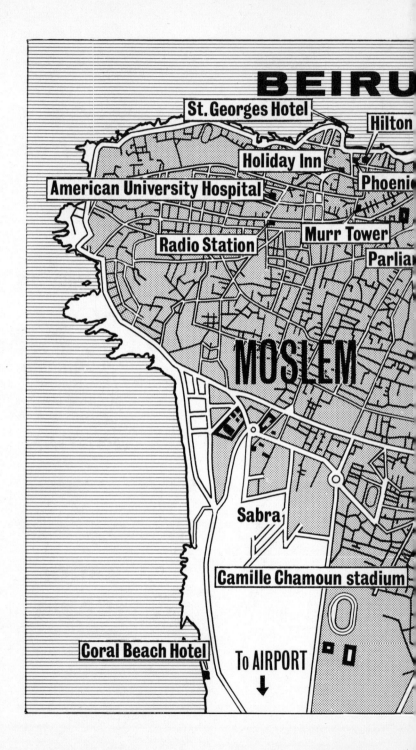

BEIRU

St. Georges Hotel

Hilton

Holiday Inn

Phoenic

American University Hospital

Murr Tower

Radio Station

Parlia

MOSLEM

Sabra

Camille Chamoun stadium

Coral Beach Hotel

To AIRPORT
↓

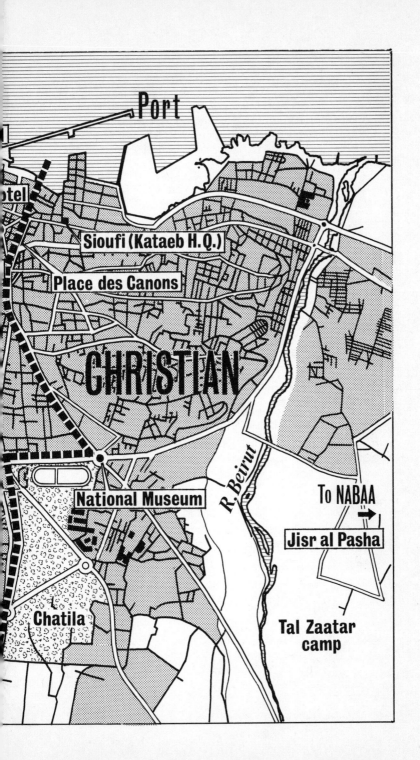